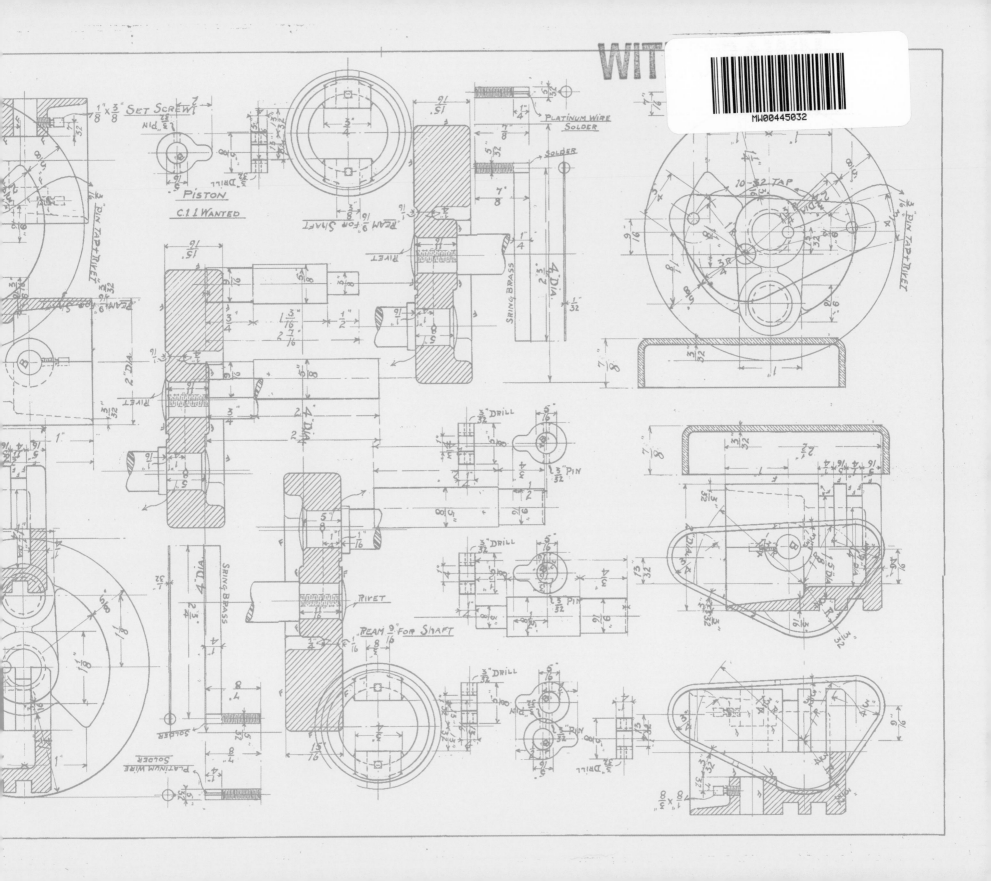

THE HARLEY-DAVIDSON STORY

TALES FROM THE ARCHIVES

THE HARLEY-DAVIDSON STORY

TALES FROM THE ARCHIVES · AARON FRANK
INTRODUCTION BY JIM FRICKE,
CURATORIAL DIRECTOR, HARLEY-DAVIDSON MUSEUM

motorbooks

Brimming with creative inspiration, how-to projects, and useful information to enrich your everyday life, Quarto Knows is a favorite destination for those pursuing their interests and passions. Visit our site and dig deeper with our books into your area of interest: Quarto Creates, Quarto Cooks, Quarto Homes, Quarto Lives, Quarto Drives, Quarto Explores, Quarto Gifts, or Quarto Kids.

JAN '19

487 7101

First published in 2018 by Motorbooks, an imprint of The Quarto Group, 401 Second Avenue North, Suite 310, Minneapolis, MN 55401 USA. T (612) 344-8100 F (612) 344-8692 www.QuartoKnows.com

Motorbooks titles are also available at discount for retail, wholesale, promotional, and bulk purchase. For details, contact the Special Sales Manager by email at specialsales@quarto.com or by mail at The Quarto Group, Attn: Special Sales Manager, 401 Second Avenue North, Suite 310, Minneapolis, MN 55401 USA.

10 9 8 7 6 5 4 3 2 1

ISBN: 978-0-7603-6071-2

Digital edition published in 2018
eISBN: 978-0-7603-6072-9

Library of Congress Control Number: 2018945210

Acquiring Editor: Zack Miller
Project Manager: Jordan Wiklund
Art Director: Laura Drew
Cover Designer: Beth Middleworth
Layout: Beth Middleworth

On the front cover: Racer Otto Walker
On the endpapers: William Harley's original motor bicycle sketches
On the front case: Walter Davidson (second from left), Arthur Davidson (center), William Davidson (center from right), with three other employees in front of the Harley-Davidson factory building circa 1909
On the back case: One of many Harley-Davidson dealer stores, circa 1916

Cushman scooter image on page 146 used with permission of Brooks Stevens Inc. Brooks Stevens (American, 1911-1995) Motor scooter, Outboard Marine Corporation (OMC), Cushman, 1960 Brooks Stevens Archive, Milwaukee Art Museum, Gift of the Brooks Stevens Family and Milwaukee Institute of Art and Design, BSA_BR_1445 • Page 196 Pictorial Press Ltd / Alamy Stock Photo

Printed in China

MIX
Paper from responsible sources
FSC® C104723
www.fsc.org

CONTENTS

INTRODUCTION

Every object has a story. Sometimes that story is obvious, right there on the surface for everyone to see. Often, divining the messages hidden within a particular object requires research, context, or specialized knowledge. But the stories are there to be found if you pay attention and know how to follow the clues.

Attempts to unlock the secrets inherent in physical objects have captivated humans for centuries. The potential of objects to inspire and to inform provides the foundation for the curator's calling: to engage the visitor in a story through careful selection, arrangement, and interpretation of artifacts.

I was lucky enough to get that job for the Harley-Davidson Museum. We began outlining the stories our exhibits would tell in 2004, and the museum was slated to open in the summer of 2008 (which it did!). The prospect of leading exhibit development for this project was both incredibly exciting and terrifying. As I familiarized myself with the fantastic collections of the Harley-Davidson Archives, my excitement about our once-in-a-lifetime endeavor grew exponentially. My concerns dissipated.

In developing this museum, our goal was to create an experience in which visitors would be guided by their individual interests and curiosity. They would make their way through a multifaceted, interwoven set of possible paths, drawn in by elements that resonate with their lives, learning new things at every turn. The effort that went into creating that experience should be invisible. To make that work, a curator must find just the right objects, integrating artifacts, photos, graphics, media, text, and environment into a seamless whole. It's never easy, and—inevitably—there are compromises when the perfect piece can't be found.

Fortunately for those of us working on the Harley-Davidson Museum, the company's founders were savers. They began preserving motorcycles, documents, printed material, and photographs just a few years after starting their business. And having set that pattern, their successors in leadership, along with generation after generation of employees, maintained the effort. Through good times and bad, booms, busts, depression and conflict, they kept adding to the ever-expanding collection.

The result of that century-plus of diligence is an unbelievable treasure trove. The vehicle collection is unparalleled and rightly gets the lion's share of attention. The photography collection is a seemingly bottomless well of beauty and information. The business documentation, marketing literature, and vintage periodicals are invaluable for research purposes, and often include just what I'm looking for to make a particular point. The various memorabilia, riding gear, and dealer and club materials reveal fascinating stories of business and recreation, use and modification, wear and repair. As we develop exhibits we consistently find the ideal artifact to support our narrative. And of course, the Archives supports a wide range of critical Motor Company initiatives.

Beyond its historical value, this collection is a physical manifestation of the pride, accomplishment, and perseverance of the people of Harley-Davidson. It's a record of the passion and creativity of the riders who have used these products to enrich their own lives and of the enthusiasts who have sustained the company through their steadfast devotion to the sport and the brand.

The Archives is a living collection. The Harley-Davidson enterprise continues and expands, and so does our collecting activity. The later chapters of this book focus on some of our more recent acquisitions. As employees of the Harley-Davidson Archives and Museum, we are proud of our roles as diligent stewards of this unparalleled collection. Generations from now, future curators and authors will be developing exhibits and writing books based on the objects we are collecting today. For the present, we hope you enjoy the stories told within these pages, and the images of the objects that inspired and illustrate the tales.

Jim Fricke
CURATORIAL DIRECTOR,
HARLEY-DAVIDSON MUSEUM

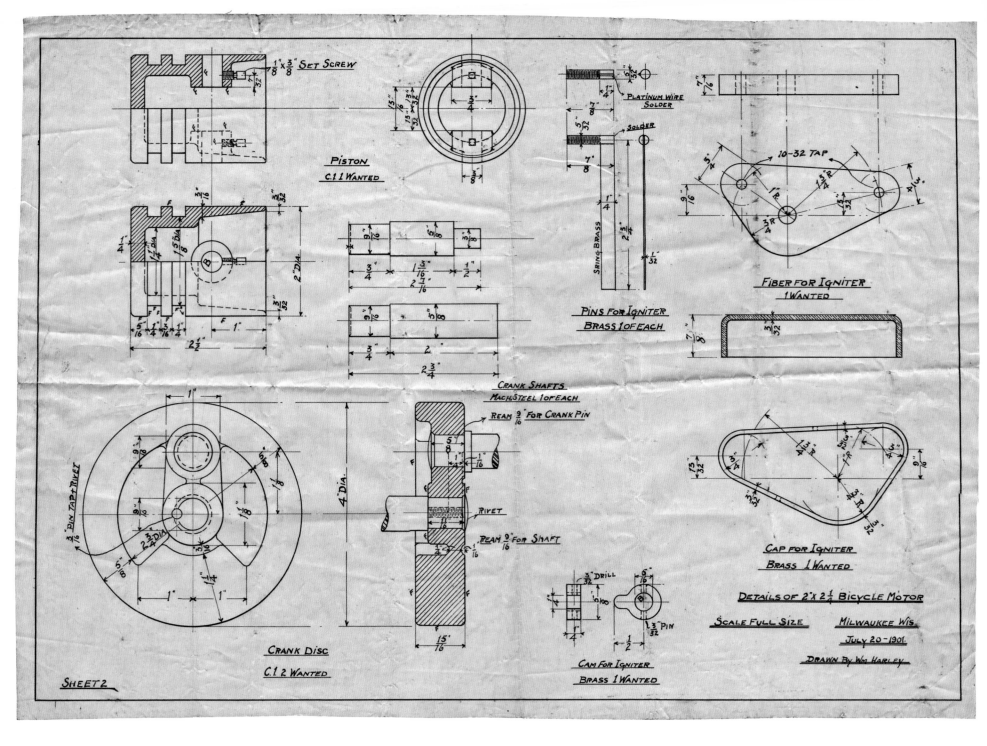

$\frac{1}{8}" \times \frac{3}{8}"$ SET SCREW

PISTON
C.I. 1 WANTED

FIBER FOR IGNITER
1 WANTED

10-32 TAP

PLATINUM WIRE
SOLDER

SOLDER

SPRING BRASS

PINS FOR IGNITER
BRASS 1 OF EACH

CRANK SHAFTS
MACH. STEEL 1 OF EACH

REAM $\frac{9}{16}$ FOR CRANK PIN

RIVET

REAM $\frac{9}{16}$ FOR SHAFT

4" DIA.

CRANK DISC
C.I. 2 WANTED

CAP FOR IGNITER
BRASS 1 WANTED

$\frac{3}{32}"$ DRILL

$\frac{3}{32}"$ PIN

CAM FOR IGNITER
BRASS 1 WANTED

DETAILS OF 2" X 2¼ BICYCLE MOTOR

SCALE FULL SIZE   MILWAUKEE WIS.

JULY 20 - 1901.

DRAWN BY WM HARLEY

SHEET 2

WILLIAM HARLEY'S BICYCLE MOTOR DRAWING

Like the name implies, the Harley-Davidson Motor Company was originally conceived of as a manufacturer of motors, to provide powerplants for bicycles, buckboards, and whatever other vehicular contrivance any industrious soul could dream up. The turn of the century was very much a time of transportation transition and expansion. The horse and buggy still ruled the roads, but any number of internal combustion-powered contraptions were attracting the attention of skilled young engineers and designers who were ready to revolutionize the wheeled world. William Harley was one such visionary.

William Harley was born and raised in Milwaukee, where he began working for a local bicycle manufacturer at the age of fifteen. By the time he was twenty-one, in 1901, he had already worked his way up to a draftsman position, where he proved himself a very talented illustrator. Harley was understandably intrigued by the possibility of a motorized bicycle, capable of traveling farther and faster than any man's two legs could go. After-hours at the bicycle

factory, Harley began sketching out concepts for his ideal version of the motorized bicycle, one of which is seen here.

This bicycle motor drawing, dated 1901, stands alone as the earliest known document in Harley-Davidson Motor Company history. As such, it acts as a sort of Rosetta Stone, revealing crucial clues about the future of the Motor Company and the founders'

dreams of reshaping transportation and personal freedom—not to mention, the burgeoning American motorcycle industry. It was this drawing that Harley used to stoke the enthusiasm of his close friend Arthur Davidson, who soon was convinced to leave a perfectly good position as a pattern maker for Ole Evinrude—the inventor of the first commercially successful outboard boat motor—to join William Harley in laying the groundwork for what would become the Motor Company.

The motorized bicycle wasn't an original idea. According to local newspaper accounts, the first motorized bicycle appeared in Milwaukee back in 1895, when Edward Joel Pennington demonstrated his "Motor Cycle" design on Wisconsin Avenue. Perhaps William Harley was among the crowd that day? Harley's engine was about the size of a modern chainsaw—displacing 7.07 cubic inches (106cc)—and it was supposedly designed with input from an unnamed "German Draftsman" whose name has since been lost to history. It took two years, and lots of assistance from his friend Henry Melk (who, crucially, owned a lathe), for Harley to complete the running prototype that debuted in the summer of

1903. The machine worked, but just barely— it reportedly struggled to summit even Milwaukee's modest hills. But this was not a failure; it was a learning experience. By that time, the first true motorcycles had arrived in Milwaukee, inspiring William Harley and Arthur Davidson to refocus their energy and apply their motorized-bicycle learnings toward developing a practical motorcycle instead.

More than anything, this simple line drawing captures an incredible moment in time. A moment when the personal transportation landscape was being rapidly and radically reshaped. A moment of incredible business opportunity, when two hard-working and resourceful young men could build a manufacturing company up from nothing, in a backyard shed. A moment when anything seemed possible, and when two good friends named William Harley and Arthur Davidson began to formulate the idea that would eventually become the Harley-Davidson Motor Company—a company that would become the most influential motorcycle manufacturer in the world.

SERIAL #1

There are so many significant motorcycles—machines that have uniquely captured the imagination or even in some small or large way actually changed the world. Lawrence of Arabia's Brough Superior SS100. Rollie Free's Vincent Black Lightning, made eternal on the pages of *Life* magazine. Peter Fonda's Harley-Davidson Panhead-based *Easy Rider* chopper. But it's not an exaggeration to claim that there is no motorcycle more important or more influential than this one, Harley-Davidson Serial Number One. No single motorcycle has launched more dreams or inspired more adventures than this one, the bike that established most important and influential motorcycle brand in the world.

More is unknown about this particular motorcycle than what is known. There exists no documentation detailing the exact history of this bike. There are very few records about any Harley-Davidson motorcycles previous to the 1907 incorporation, in fact—the founders were too busy altering the transportation landscape to pay attention to boring details such as production notes. It's commonly understood that William Harley and Arthur Davidson built three complete motorcycles in 1903 and 1904, though accounts of the build dates of those first bikes are often confused and more often merged. It's doubtful that this

motorcycle represents the first—there were likely at least one or maybe two unmarked prototypes before it—but with major engine components clearly marked with the number 001, this is certainly the oldest known Harley-Davidson and one of a literal handful of pre-1905 Harley-Davidsons that still exist today.

No one knows how much of what is today called Serial Number One is original or even true. For instance, we have no idea what this bike looked like when it first rolled out of the workshop behind the Davidson family home at 38th and Highland in Milwaukee, Wisconsin. What we do know is that by the late 1910s Harley-Davidson was actively buying back earlier models and building replicas of its earliest motorcycles, using period parts. This is believed to have been one of those replicas (the frame is not original, dating to 1905).

We do know that at one point this bike was dressed up for show and made to resemble a bike from the 1905–1908 period, complete with many incorrect details, including fenders, pin-striped paint, and bar-and-shield logos that likely didn't even exist until 1908. This is what Serial Number One looked like when it was first restored in the 1970s.

A second restoration was undertaken in 1996, with the intent to make the motorcycle as original as possible. That's when it was returned to the condition that you see here, with the Harley-Davidson logo on the left side of the tank only, with the correct handlebars, no fenders, and numerous other details that correspond with what little we do know about Harley-Davidson's very first bikes.

The Thomas B. Jeffery Company
Of Illinois.

Chicago, Ill., April 15th, 1912.

Harley-Davidson Motor Co.,
  Mr. C. H. Lang, Ill. Distributor,
    Chicago, Illinois.

Dear Sir:-

When I bought my Harley-Davidson Motorcycle, which I still have in daily use, it had already run 51,000 miles.

According to my information it is the first Harley-Davidson that was ever built. It was made in 1903 and sold in 1904 to Mr. Mayer of Milwaukee who rode it 6,000 miles. Geo. W. Lyon of Chicago rode it 15,000 miles. Dr. Webster of Rush Medical College of Chicago rode it 18,000 miles. Louis Fluke rode it 12,000 miles.

I bought this machine from Louis Fluke in 1907 and have ridden it to date 32,000 miles, which makes a total of 83,000 miles. It is in perfect condition and still has the same main bearings.

It has a 3 1-4 H.P. motor and 25.94 cubic inches piston displacement, the largest sized motor used in motorcycles at that time.

I am repairman for the Thomas B. Jeffery Company the Chicago branch where the Rambler automobiles are sold and kept in repair. I make trips with my machine to repair cars, if they get into trouble out in the country.

I also use it daily to and from work, besides using it during business hours. It has given me entire satisfaction as it is always on the job and always makes good when called upon for service.

The new Harley-Davidson now has wonderful improvements over my old model, but I would not like to sell it, because it has stood by me rain or shine. It is now nine years in service and will make good for many more years.

Yours very truly,

Steve J Sparough

THE HARLEY-DAVIDSON DEALER

MAKES CLAIM OF RECORD

Stephen E. Sparough's 1903 Harley-Davidson Has Covered 83,000 Miles and Is Anxious for More.

That Harley-Davidson machines give good service year after year is shown by the letter on the opposite page received by C. H. Lang, Chicago dealer. Steve J. Sparough, an expert repairman employed by the Thomas B. Jeffery company, boasts a 1903 Harley-Davidson machine that has made 83,000 miles and that is good for many more thousands of miles.

The 3¼ horsepower motor is still in perfect condition. At the earnest solicitation of Mr. Lang the old-timer was permitted by Mr. Sparough to visit its birthplace.

What it saw there is a remarkable story—as remarkable as the performance of this old veteran of the city pavement and the country road—and would well merit the attention of any good biographer.

HIS HARLEY-DAVIDSON IS ALWAYS READY WHEN HE WANTS IT.

WHEN Walter Wallenthin, of Attleboro, Mass., received his first motorcycle, a 1911 Harley-Davidson, it looked so neat and trim that he hesitated to take it out on the dirty roads, but when he had overcome that feeling he wished that he had obtained his machine earlier.

"I found the Harley-Davidson just what I wanted it to be, quiet and quick and clean," says Mr. Wallenthin. "I used it every day to and from my work and took many pleasure rides with it out from Attleboro. It always started with the first stroke of the pedal down, which surprised the town people very much. I used the free engine device to show the public the advantage of it in crowded places where a quick stop is needed. It worked great—much better than other free engine clutches.

Just Trying the Seat

"My machine was a battery model, but I only used one set of batteries in 1911 and they were five amperes at that. The cost of the batteries for a season's run was 75 cents. I have had no tire trouble whatever, and no trouble with the engine or belt, or any other part. My Harley-Davidson is always ready when I want it. The cost of gasoline and oil is hardly noticeable. If I was to figure out trips I made in cars and trains, it would almost buy a new machine.

"I used it for towing in motorcycles of other makes without showing any labor on the machine.

As near as I can calculate I traveled fifteen hundred miles in 1911 on my Harley-Davidson. I rode it until December 30th, when it snowed for the first time here in the East.

"My 1911 model looks so new that my agent asked me what kind of polishing rags I used. I told him I used soft flannel rags, which do not scratch the nickel or enamel.

"No parts have become loose or broken, and no noise heard anywhere. It was the first real motorcycle I ever owned. I only hope my 1912 Harley-Davidson will have as good a record for durability and low cost of operation."

The frame configuration is what really separates the first Harley-Davidson motorcycle from the motorized bicycles that preceded it. The engine and the frame are specifically designed to fit together on a true motorcycle, a mandatory arrangement to accommodate the larger engine and flywheel necessary to deliver the performance and reliability that was required by even the earliest motorcycle consumers. And so the diamond-type bicycle frame has been abandoned here in favor of the so-called "loop frame," with its front downtube that wraps elegantly around the lower engine case to provide a lower center of gravity and increased rigidity. Though motorcycle design at this early stage is entirely functional, the loop frame also has the unintended effect of positioning the engine like a gem in a setting—a key styling element that still influences Harley-Davidson motorcycles today.

Much like his early motor-bicycle designs, William Harley's first motorcycle was inspired by contemporaries in what was already a crowded motorcycle market. Manufacturers such as Marsh, Curtiss, and Indian, even other Wisconsin makers such as Merkel, also made in Milwaukee, and Mitchell in nearby Racine, were already well established in 1903. The basic architecture of Serial Number One is similar to the loop-framed Merkel in many ways. The single-cylinder engine is quite similar to the same-vintage Evinrude outboard, not surprising since Arthur Davidson had spent some years working for Ole Evinrude. The atmospheric-valve single displaces 24.27 cubic inches (405cc), with a 9¾-inch flywheel attached to a 28-pound crankshaft, and final drive is a hand-tensioned leather belt. There is no transmission or clutch—Harley-Davidson was the first American manufacturer

to offer a clutch, but not until 1907. Everything is designed to be simple and reliable, which is all that was required of a motorcycle in those early days.

What, if anything, might we assume about this very unassuming single-cylinder machine with no lights, no fenders, and what is estimated to be just a 40-mile-per-hour top speed? One theory suggests that Serial Number One was a prototype, supported by the fact that the specifications of this engine don't match anything known about the earliest production Harley-Davidson engines. Another theory suggests that this bike was built for competition, since it was discovered during the most recent restoration that this is an unusually high-compression engine. It's reported that a rider named Edward Hildebrand finished fourth in a motorcycle race at Wisconsin State Fair Park on September 8, 1904—one of the first documented appearances of a Harley-Davidson motorcycle in the popular press—could he have been riding a motorcycle powered by this very engine?

No one knows for sure if the humble Serial Number One, purpose-built but barely more sophisticated than a contemporary motorized bicycle, was intended to change the world. Walter Davidson claimed that the first Harley-Davidson motorcycle was built purely for personal use, little more than a plaything to amuse his brother Arthur and his best friend William Harley. Mostly, the duo just wanted to improve on their crude motor-bicycle design, which they considered underperforming and even unsafe. But once they witnessed the potential of this new motorcycle design—and more importantly, once members of the general public saw it in action and began clambering for one of their own—William Harley and Arthur Davidson found themselves genuine motorcycle manufacturers. In the same year that Henry Ford produced his first automobile and the Wright brothers completed their first successful powered flight, Harley-Davidson built and sold its first motorcycle. And the firm hasn't looked back since.

CHICAGO MOTORCYCLE CLUB TROPHY

William Harley and Arthur Davidson were true motorcycle enthusiasts—not just opportunity-seeking entrepreneurs—so it's not surprising that even in the company's earliest days they were interested in competition. But it wasn't until Arthur's brother Walter joined the company that Harley-Davidson really made its mark on the racing world. Walter's real passion was riding motorcycles, not just making them, and his unstoppable enthusiasm for speed quickly cemented Harley-Davidson's reputation for quality and performance.

This modest silver cup, presented to Walter Davidson on July 4, 1905, marks the occasion of his winning the Chicago Motorcycle Club's Ten Mile Open—his first racing victory at a national-level event. As the reliability and performance of Harley-Davidson motorcycles continued to improve, Walter ventured further afield to participate in more prestigious events. His most important victory came in 1908, when he won the seventh annual Federation of American Motorcyclists (FAM) Endurance and Reliability Run, held in New York's Catskill Mountains. Achieving a

perfect score of 1,000 points over the two-day, 356-mile route, Walter beat sixty-five other riders on seventeen different makes of motorcycle—including the best European bikes—to clearly establish the superiority of Harley-Davidson motorcycles.

The rivalry brewing between upstart Harley-Davidson and then-dominant Indian made Walter's New York victory especially satisfying. That Walter Davidson completed the endurance run entirely unsupported—in stark contrast to the Indian factory

THE CENTER SPREAD
OF THE 1909 CATALOG
SHOWCASING VARIOUS
RACING TROPHIES AND
AWARDS WON BY HARLEY-
DAVIDSON MOTORCYCLES.

effort, which included company founders George Hendee and Oscar Hedstrom following in a backup car packed full of tools and spare parts—made it even sweeter. For an encore three days later, Walter Davidson earned first-place in the FAM Economy Contest, traveling 50 miles on 1 quart and 1 ounce of gas. Judges were so impressed that they awarded Davidson five bonus points for consistency and overall excellence.

Walter Davidson's FAM Diamond Medal figured prominently in Harley-Davidson's 1909 advertisements. Each racing win was an incontrovertible endorsement that boosted the reputation of the Harley-Davidson brand. But just a few years later, there was an intense public backlash against motorcycle racing. Board-track racing had become one of America's most popular spectator sports, with big races attracting more than ten thousand fans. Just as quickly, it became America's deadliest sport. Brakeless bikes roaring around oil-soaked wooden raceways, just inches apart at more than 100 miles per hour, inevitably resulted in horrific accidents. Hundreds of lives—racers and spectators both—were being lost annually, and motorcycle racing was soon something that major motorcycle manufacturers, Harley-Davidson included, actively distanced themselves from.

"We are building motorcycles to be used by sane people for pleasure and for business. We do not want our machines ridden by lunatics," read a statement in *The Harley-Davidson Dealer* in September 1913. Officially, the Harley-Davidson Motor Company didn't support or participate in racing. But even while the Motor Company publically disapproved of racing, it couldn't ignore the fact that racing sold bikes. Soon enough, Harley-Davidson advertisements were boasting under-the-table racing victories accomplished "without our assistance."

Arthur Davidson had penned strongly worded anti-racing articles as late as 1913, so it was quite a surprise when, at the very last minute, Harley-Davidson entered the Dodge City 300 in Dodge City, Kansas, in July 1914. Though they entered under the wire, Harley-Davidson had been secretly preparing for this race for at least a year. The Motor Company showed up in Dodge City with an all-new V-twin race bike (the 11-K), along with a five-man factory racing team—this was the birth of Harley-Davidson's legendary Wrecking Crew. Though Harley-Davidson didn't win at Dodge City in 1914— Indian took the victory that year—the Wrecking Crew dominated that event in 1915 and 1916, and pretty much every other prestigious American racing event for many years to come.

Davidson and Turner Share Honors.

Walter Davidson, of Milwaukee, and J. A. Turner of the Chicago Motor Cycle Club, carried off all the honors at the race meet of that organization, held on the half-mile track at Crown Point, Ind., Thursday, 4th inst. Davidson and Turner each landed two firsts in fast times. Two thousand persons witnessed the races, which were run off without a hitch, the feature being a ten mile pursuit between Turner and H. Walters of the Milwaukee Motorcycle Club, which the former won in 15 minutes 30 seconds. The summaries:

One mile open—Won by Walter Davidson (Harley Davidson); second, Paul Hildebrand; third, George W. Lyons. Time, 1:34⅘.

Three mile open—Won by J. A. Turner (Armac); second, Walter Davidson; third, Fred Blankenheim. Time, 4:35.

Five mile open—Won by Walter Davidson; second, W. L. Walsh; third, J. A. Turner. Time, 7:32.

Ten mile pursuit between J. A. Turner, C. M. C., and H. Walters, Milwaukee M. C.—Won by Turner. Time 15:30.

HOLDS STATE MOTOR CYCLE RECORD

HARLEY-DAVIDSON MOTOR CO.

Space No. 41—Armory Gallery
C. H. LANG, Representative,
15 E. ADAMS. ST.

YALE CALIFORNIA CYCLES.

WALTER DAVIDSON
Winner of Motorcycle Race on Harley-Davidson.

Pope-Hartford Driver Makes Clean Sweep in Automobile Derby at State Fair Park.

DEFEATS BARNEY OLDFIELD

Famous Driver Takes Novelty Race in Which All Other Starters Are Disqualified.

THREE MILES

Free-for-all. Standing start. H. B. Lusher Cup.
Sanctioned by the F. A. M.

Owner.	Driver.
Louis Hall	Louis Hall
Adolph Wicknick	Adolph Wicknick
A. T. Wilson	A. T. Wilson
Wm. H. Roberts	Wm. C. Rumford
John Bender	John Bender
Harry Witham	Harry Witham
Alex. Klein	Alex. Klein
A. L. Hilaman	A. L. Hilaman
E. T. Banes	E. T. Banes
H. L. Ellis	H. L. Ellis
S. W. Kresser	S. W. Kresser
David Cullen	D. Cullen

Meeting of the Board of Directors.

Immediately following the adjournment of the first stockholders' meeting of the Corporation, the Board of Directors of said Corporation elected at said meeting met at _3800_ _Chestnut St_ City of _Milwaukee_ State of _Wisconsin_ on the _17th_ day of _Sept_ at _8_ o'clock _P_ m.

The meeting was called to order by _Walter Davidson_ and its object stated.

Chairman and Secretary Elected.

On motion, duly made and carried, _Walter Davidson_ was elected Chairman, and _Arthur Davidson_ was elected Secretary of the meeting.

Directors Present.

The Chairman then instructed the Secretary to read the list of Directors, and the following Directors were found to be present:

Wm S Harley
Walter Davidson
Wm A Davidson
Arthur Davidson

Election of Officers.

A quorum being present, on motion, duly made and carried, the Board proceeded to the election of officers of the Corporation to serve for the ensuing fiscal year.

On motion, duly made and carried, the following were elected to the office of—

President _Walter Davidson_
Vice-President _Wm S Harley_
Secretary _Arthur Davidson_
Treasurer _Arthur Davidson_

Seal.

On motion, duly made and carried, the following resolution was adopted:

Resolved, That the Secretary be instructed to procure a seal having the following words shown thereon by the impression thereof _Harley Davidson Motor Co. Milwaukee Wis_

and the same is adopted as the corporate seal of this corporation, and the Secretary is hereby directed to take an impression upon the margin of the page of the records upon which this resolution shall be recorded for the purpose of future identification.

On motion, duly made and carried, the following resolution was adopted:

Stock Certificates.

Resolved, That the Secretary be instructed to purchase a book of stock certificates, to be issued upon subscription to the capital stock of this Corporation.

Committee on By-Laws.

On motion, duly made and carried, a committee consisting of—

The Board of Directors

were appointed to prepare a form of By-Laws for the government of the affairs of the Corporation, and present the same to the Board of Directors for consideration at the earliest possible moment.

On motion, duly made and carried, the following resolution was adopted:

Treasurer's Bond.

Resolved, That the Treasurer be and is hereby directed to execute and deliver to the Corporation a bond in the sum of_____dollars, with_____sureties to be approved by this Board, conditioned that he will account for all moneys and property that may come into his hands as Treasurer of this Corporation, as required by the By-Laws.

On motion, duly made and carried, the following resolution was adopted:

Payment for Stock.

Resolved, That the sum of _One hundred_ dollars on each and every share subscribed to the capital stock of this Corporation be paid to the Treasurer by the subscribers thereof respectively on or before the _17th_ day of _Sept_ 19__.

File of Charter.

On motion, duly made and carried, the Secretary was instructed to file the charter or articles of incorporation for public record, in accordance with the statutes in such case made and provided.

Blank Books and Stationery.

On motion, duly made and carried, the Secretary was instructed to procure, at the expense of the Corporation, all the necessary stationery, blank books, etc., for the use of the Corporation.

Adoption of By-Laws.

The committee appointed to prepare a form for By-Laws presented its report, with a code of By-Laws, which was, on motion, duly made and carried, adopted and ordered spread upon the minutes and the committee discharged.

Payment of Bills.

On motion, duly made and carried, the Secretary was instructed to draw an order on the Treasurer for the payment of all bills for the expenses of incorporating and for the seal, stock certificates, records, etc.

On motion, duly made and carried, the following resolution was adopted:

Resolved, That until further action of this Board upon this subject, the Treasurer is instructed to pay out no money on account of this Corporation, except upon orders drawn by the Secretary and countersigned by the President.

On motion, duly made and carried, the meeting adjourned to_____ _7th_ day of _October_ 19__.

Walter Davidson
President.

Attest:

Arthur Davidson
Secretary.

4

ARTICLES OF INCORPORATION

William Harley and Arthur Davidson built their first motorcycle in 1903. By the next year, after making numerous technical improvements, they were firmly in the business of making motorcycles. Harley and Davidson placed their first advertisement in a magazine called *Horseless Age* in 1905, followed shortly by another in the *Automobile and Cycle Trade Journal*, offering bare engines for sale. That same year, the first Harley-Davidson dealer, Carl H. Lang of Chicago, sold three complete motorcycles—60 percent of that year's total production. The company produced ten times as many bikes in 1906—around fifty total—employing six men full time, working in a new, 2,880-square-foot factory located on what was then Chestnut Street (now Juneau Avenue), just a block from the Davidson family home where the original workshop stood. With Harley-Davidson driven forward by this momentum, the year 1907 proved a turning point for the company. This is the year that Harley-Davidson went from being a productive hobby to a fully formed and functioning corporation.

THE ORIGINAL HARLEY-DAVIDSON MOTOR COMPANY SHED IN THE BACKYARD OF THE DAVIDSON FAMILY HOME AT 38TH AND HIGHLAND.

Harley-Davidson Motor Company became a legal corporation on Sept. 17, 1907. Look closely at the articles of incorporation signed on that date and note that these aren't carefully crafted legal documents, but, rather, simple declarations entered into a do-it-yourself incorporation manual published and sold by a local Milwaukee stationary store. The mere existence of a fill-in-the-blank incorporation manual says a lot about Milwaukee at the turn of the last century. Known then as "The Machine Shop of the World," Milwaukee's Menomonee Valley was smokestacks as far as the eye could see thanks to countless workshops, mills, and foundries located within the Milwaukee city limits. This made Milwaukee the ideal place to start a motorcycle manufacturing

company. The do-it-yourself incorporation manual is evidence of the powerful entrepreneurial spirit that defined Milwaukee at the time of Harley-Davidson's birth.

The Harley-Davidson Motor Company has four founding fathers: William S. Harley, Arthur Davidson, Walter Davidson, and William A. Davidson. William Harley and Arthur Davidson, of course, were in it from the beginning. Walter Davidson joined the effort late in 1903, leaving his former position as a railroad machinist. William A. Davidson was the last to join, just prior to incorporation. He was another ex-railroad worker, having most recently served as tool room foreman for the Milwaukee Road. His first task for the newly

THE ORIGINAL SHED WITH THE 1904
ADDITION, STILL IN THE YARD OF THE
DAVIDSON FAMILY HOME AT 38TH AND
HIGHLAND.

OPPOSITE: WILLIAM
HARLEY (SECOND FROM
LEFT), WALTER DAVIDSON
(FOURTH FROM LEFT),
AND ARTHUR DAVIDSON
(FAR RIGHT) ON THE
PORCH OF THEIR CABIN
ON LAKE RIPLEY, NEAR
CAMBRIDGE, WISCONSIN,
CIRCA 1905.

founded corporation was to oversee purchase of the machining tools and presses that helped the young company meet the ever-expanding demand for motorcycles.

Walter Davidson was named the first president of Harley-Davidson Motor Company and the first chairman of the board too. (Other members of the inaugural board included engineer Henry Melk, dealer C. H. Lang, and business advisor Frank Woods.) William Harley served a dual role as chief engineer and treasurer, positions he held until his death in 1943. Arthur—the youngest of the three Davidson brothers—was the driving force behind setting up Harley-Davidson's dealer network, both nationally and internationally, and he also oversaw the Motor Company's early advertising efforts. William Davidson—the eldest of the three Davidson brothers, affectionately known around the factory as "Old Bill"—managed manufacturing operations and hiring.

The initial stock shares are also on display at the museum. Company stock was split four ways among the four founders, but it wasn't split equally. William Harley structured his portion of the deal to receive more cash than stock, in order to pay for his newly minted engineering degree from the University of Wisconsin at Madison. (Harley was the only of the four founders to hold a college degree.) Remaining shares were made public and sold mostly to family members and other employees, at the cost of $100 per share. The initial capital investment in the newly founded corporation was about $35,000—the bulk of which was used to finance a second-floor expansion at the just-completed Chestnut Street factory.

The original mission statement of the Harley-Davidson Motor Company—"Manufacture and sell motorcycles, motors, marine engines, and fixtures, and appliances"—is interesting to consider.

1904 PROMISSORY NOTE FOR $170 FROM JAMES MCLAY (AKA "HONEY UNCLE")

Did company founders envision more than just a motorcycle company? There are no records of Harley-Davidson having ever produced a marine engine, and it's not known how many individual engines the Motor Company ever sold. The museum has displayed some unusual Harley-Davidson-powered "appliances," including a V-twin-powered mining cart, a V-twin ice saw, and even a motorized canvas sled—an early snowmobile—but it's not clear whether these engines were purchased directly from the Motor Company for these purposes or if they were repurposed from unused or discarded motorcycles. Regardless of the founders' original intentions, Harley-Davidson became almost immediately and exclusively a producer of motorcycles only.

The newly formed corporation was successful at once. Within five years, by 1912, that two-story wooden workshop would be replaced with a six-story, 300,000-square-foot red brick factory capable of producing tens of thousands of motorcycles per year. The story of Harley-Davidson had become a full-blown fairy tale: "Nowhere

in the world of romance can there be found a more fascinating tale than that which tells of the beginnings and the subsequent phenomenal growth of the H-D Motor Co., Milwaukee. This, our country, is indeed the land of opportunity—the history of Harley-Davidson Company proves that," proclaimed a story in the March 31, 1914, issue of the *Milwaukee Journal*, celebrating the Motor Company's runaway success.

Four uniquely strong talents built Harley-Davidson Motor Company from the ground up—and it's worth noting that all four founders stayed deeply involved and invested in day-to-day business operations for more than thirty years, through the ends of their respective careers. The four founders were motorcycle enthusiasts first, mostly self-taught and with little practical engineering, marketing, or business experience—but filled with enthusiasm and sharing one very big dream. That dream became a reality in 1907, when these incorporation documents were signed, and the Harley-Davidson Motor Company has been on the gas ever since.

MINUTES OF THE FIRST MEETING OF STOCKHOLDERS OF THE
HARLEY-DAVIDSON MOTOR COMPANY.

A meeting of the stockholders of the Harley-Davidson
Motor Company was held on the 17th day of September, 1907, at
8 o'clock P.M., at the office of said Company, 3800 Chestnut
Street, in the City of Milwaukee, in the State of Wisconsin.

All incorporators or subscribers to stock named in
the Articles of Organization were present, namely: Wm. S.
Harley, Walter Davidson, Wm. A. Davidson and Arthur Davidson.

Mr. Walter Davidson called the meeting to order.

On motion of Mr. Wm. S. Harley, seconded by Mr. Wm.
A. Davidson, Mr. Walter Davidson was unanimously elected chairman of the meeting, and Arthur Davidson secretary.

A waiver of notice of the time and place and purpose
of the first meeting of the stockholders signed by all stockholders was presented and read to the meeting and ordered to be
spread upon the minutes by the Secretary as follows:

We, the subscribers, being all the parties named in
the certificate of organization of the Harley-Davidson Motor
Company, do hereby waive notice of the time, place and purpose
of the first meeting of said Company, and do fix this 17th
day of September, A. D. 1907, at 8 o'clock in the afternoon
as the time and the office of the Harley-Davidson Motor Co.,
3800 Chestnut Street, in the city of Milwaukee, State of
Wisconsin, as the place of the first meeting of said Company.

Dated September ..17th..,1907.

(Signatures by all the Incorporators.)

(I am sending this waiver of notice on a separate
sheet to be signed and filed with the secretary so that the

5

FIRST V-TWIN MOTORCYCLE

It's almost impossible today to imagine a Harley-Davidson motorcycle powered by anything but a V-twin engine. It's been since 1978, when the single-cylinder SX250 was last offered for sale, that anything other than a V-twin motorcycle has been available with the bar-and-shield logo on the tank. "The V-twin engine is the heartbeat of everything we do," says former Chief Styling Officer Willie G. Davidson, and indeed the V-twin engine configuration has come to define Harley-Davidson motorcycles. The V-twin even determines the signature sound of a Harley-Davidson, the distinctive "potato-potato-potato" exhaust note that is so unmistakable that the Motor Company even attempted (unsuccessfully) to trademark it in the 1990s.

Harley-Davidson didn't invent the V-twin motorcycle. Glenn Curtiss, another American motorcycle and aviation pioneer, built the first V-twin motorcycle in 1903. Press reports suggest that Harley-Davidson was experimenting with V-twin engines as early as 1907—and one competed in a Chicago-area hillclimb in 1908—but the Motor Company didn't debut its first production V-twin powerplant until 1909. The ever-increasing demand for more power and speed had stretched Harley-Davidson's existing single-cylinder engines to their limit, straining both reliability and comfort. Adding a second cylinder would not only boost power output, but also reduce stress on the engine and increase rider comfort by decreasing vibration. Adding a V-twin to the lineup would also be a competitive advantage, since archrival Indian Motocycle had been selling V-twins since 1906.

Harley-Davidson created its first V-twin by simply joining two single-cylinder engines on a common crankshaft and engine cases. A narrow, 45-degree V-angle kept the new engine compact, so it could fit into the existing loop frame used for single-cylinder models. This hastily constructed V-twin was a complete failure. Complications with the crude atmospheric intake valves, which functioned poorly when sharing a single intake tract between two cylinders, resulted in a V-twin that was no faster than the single it was supposed to replace and less reliable too. The Motor Company promptly discontinued the V-twin motor after one year and went back to the drawing board.

When the 1911 model year rolled around, Harley-Davidson was ready with a hugely improved V-twin, now with mechanically operated intake valves (using pushrods) that allowed higher engine speeds and produced more power. The all-new, 49.5-cubic-inch V-twin produced 11 reliable horsepower—enough to charge over steep hills and achieve a top speed of nearly 65 miles per hour. Buyers responded enthusiastically, and Harley-Davidson scrambled to keep up with the demand. Production more than tripled, and by March of 1913, the Juneau Avenue plant was turning out one new bike every seven minutes; by 1914, that interval shrunk to just five minutes and thirty seconds for a total production of twenty thousand motorcycles that year—the majority of which were V-twins.

The new V-twin engine was so successful that Harley-Davidson discontinued its single-cylinder offerings entirely in 1918. Harley-Davidson's basic F-head V-twin carried the company for the nearly two decades, powering success on the battlefields during World War I and claiming some of Harley-Davidson's greatest racing victories during the 1920s. At the time, it seemed like the V-twin-powered Wrecking Crew was utterly unbeatable. This run continued until 1929, when the venerable F-head was replaced with the first 45-cubic-inch flathead V-twin, another legendary engine configuration that stayed in production—remarkably—through 1973.

The V-twin engine was originally favored for its mechanical attributes—compact arrangement, efficient power output, and reliable operation. Those attributes are constant, but for fans of the Harley-Davidson brand, the V-twin engine has since come to be valued as much or more for its aesthetic appeal, and the sculptural beauty it presents when fit perfectly into the frame, resting like a jewel in a setting. Other engine configurations might come and go, but for Harley-Davidson, the 45-degree V-twin engine will always remain an iconic stylistic signature and a point of pride.

1911 F-Head

IGNITION TROUBLES SPEED
MISSING AT LOW SPEED

SPARK PLUG POINTS TOO CLOSE
DEFECTIVE SPARK PLUG
CUTOUT SWITCH NOT CLOSING PROPERLY
WEAK BATTERY AND TOO MANY LIGHTS BURNING
LOOSE CONNECTION BETWEEN THE COIL AND
CIRCUIT BREAKER SCREWS TRY SCREW
IN BREAKER HOUSING
TUNGSTEN WORK OFF OF LEVER AND SCREW
(POINTS MAY BE LOOSE) SPARKING
CIRCUIT BREAKER BASE OILY AND DIRTY.—
NO GROUND CONTACT. NOTE! SPARKING
WILL BE NOTICEABLE AT CONTROL
LEVER.
TIMER HOUSING NOT SECURED TO
END PLATE WITH SET SCREW.
DEFECTIVE COIL.
DEFECTIVE CONDENSER.

MISSING AT HIGH SPEED

ANY OF ABOVE FAULTS.
WEAK BRUSH SPRINGS
WEAK CONTACT LEVER SPRING
CRYSTALLIZED TUNGSTEN POINTS
ANY CAUSE THAT WILL ALL VOLTAGE TO
RAISE: LOOSE BATTERY CONNECTIONS
DOOR, SWITCH ADI. NO WATER IN BATT.
AND LOOSE TERMINALS
INTERMITTENT SHORT CIRCUITS
IN GEN. OR IGNITION WIRING.

CARBURETOR TROUBLES ALL MAY APPEAR TO BE IGNITION TROUBLES

CIRCUIT BREAKER PARTS

GROUND REDDISH X DISCONNECT TO GENERATOR

SPACER

HORN

300 MILES OR FULLY CHARGED BATTERY 1100 CHARGING

CONNECTS CABLE DRY STORAGE OR TEST DIRECT ON TEST OF COIL BATTERY TYPE TERMINAL

DISCONNECT THE RED+WIRE AND GROUND IT

DISCONNECT WIRE FROM REAR END OF COIL

JOE RYAN SERVICE NOTEBOOKS

Yes, there really is a Harley-Davidson University, and no, you cannot enroll to earn a master's degree in motorcycology—unless you are a Harley-Davidson corporate or Harley-Davidson dealer employee. Harley-Davidson University—known as the Harley-Davidson Service School until the late 1990s—is where employees go for specialized sales or service training. And though it now serves Harley-Davidson employees at every level from dealership technician to internal sales staff, Harley-Davidson University was originally created in 1917 specifically to train military mechanics during the run-up to America's involvement in World War I.

More than half of Harley-Davidson's 1917 production was earmarked for the military, and almost immediately Arthur Davidson realized the need to train military mechanics to maintain motorcycles on the battlefield. In July of 1917, nine corporals traveled from Fort Sam Houston in Texas to Harley-Davidson's Juneau Avenue headquarters, where they participated in a three-week intensive training program. The Harley-Davidson Quartermasters School, as it was then known, was born.

It didn't take long for Arthur Davidson to recognize the value of this training program as a tool to support the ever-expanding number of Harley-Davidson dealers across the country. After World War I ended, the name changed to the Harley-Davidson Service School and enrollment opened, tuition free, to any authorized Harley-Davidson dealership employee.

An ambitious factory mechanic, Joseph Ray Ryan, was promoted to direct the first Service School some time shortly after his hiring in 1919—a position he would hold for more than four decades, until his eventual retirement from the Motor Company in 1963. Ryan is a true unsung hero of the Harley-Davidson story, and his uncompromising work ethic, his tireless enthusiasm, and his unwavering dedication to excellence played a key role in shaping the Harley-Davidson brand. Ryan personally mentored thousands of dealers and mechanics during his long professional career—issuing personal advice, writing letters of recommendation, even occasionally providing financial support—and as such has left an enduring legacy that reaches far beyond the walls of Juneau Avenue, touching nearly every aspect of the American motorcycle industry today.

The Harley-Davidson Museum counts many pieces of Ryan-related memorabilia among its collection, but nothing captures Ryan's commitment to his position more than his personal notebooks, two of which are showcased on display. Dating from the 1920s, these leather-bound notebooks contain page after page of remarks and materials that Ryan referred to during classroom lectures, as well as painstakingly accurate technical drawings—many finished with colored pencils—that revealed Ryan's equal talent as an illustrator.

Ryan served other roles at Harley-Davidson too, managing the parts department and also working as a mechanic for the factory racing team—the museum exhibit showcases a photo of Ryan trackside at Baltimore-Washington Speedway in 1925, tuning for Wrecking Crew racer Jim Davis—but he is more frequently represented in front of a classroom full of students, or posing with a graduating class for the traditional group portrait in front of the Juneau Avenue factory.

Ryan understood the importance of the Service School and the role that his graduates played in elevating the ownership experience for every Harley-Davidson customer—an impact that went far beyond just keeping the motorcycle in excellent running order. "We are not satisfied just to have sold you a motorcycle," Ryan wrote during his early days at the Service School. "We want you to get full enjoyment, pleasure, and usefulness from your Harley-Davidson. That means to furnish parts, to make repairs, to give advice, and perform many other duties embodied and understood by the word 'service.'" Over the course of his tenure, Ryan steadily increased the scope of the Service School to incorporate sales seminars, management training, even special programming for those who maintained commercial vehicles, police motorcycles, and even golf carts during the years when Harley-Davidson manufactured those.

Joe Ryan's Service School constantly evolved to suit the needs of a motorcycle company that was likewise constantly changing. Judging from the numerous student records contained in the museum archives—and the many personal thank you notes penned to Mr. Ryan from grateful Service School graduates—Ryan's rigorous evaluations were very influential. Generations of dealer principles learned their craft under his watchful eye, and it's not any exaggeration to suggest that Joe Ryan—and the knowledge contained in this little black book—was an enormous influence in building Harley-Davidson into the respected brand that it is today.

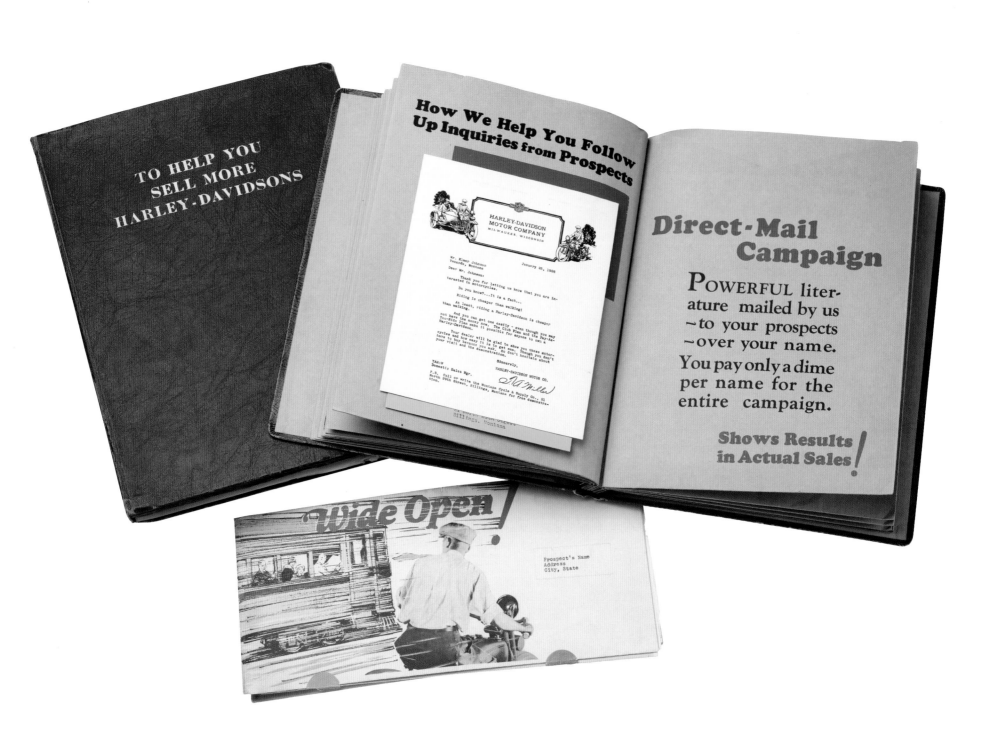

**TO HELP YOU
SELL MORE
HARLEY-DAVIDSONS**

**How We Help You Follow
Up Inquiries from Prospects**

HARLEY-DAVIDSON
MOTOR COMPANY
MILWAUKEE, WISCONSIN

January 25, 1926

Mr. Elmer Johnson
Vananda, Montana

Dear Mr. Johnson:

Thank you for letting us know that you are interested in motorcycles.

Do you know?...It is a fact...

Riding is cheaper than walking!

At least, riding a Harley-Davidson is cheaper
than walking!

And you can get one easily - even though you may
not have the money now. The Club Plan and the Pay-As-
You-Ride Plan make it possible for anyone to own a
Harley-Davidson.

Your dealer will be glad to show you these motorcycles - and how easy it is to get one. Though you don't
have to buy because you ask. So don't hesitate about
your visit and the demonstration.

Sincerely,

HARLEY-DAVIDSON MOTOR CO.

TAM:W
Domestic Sales Mgr.

P.S. Call or write the Montana Cycle & Supply Co., 21
North 29th Street, Billings, Montana for free demonstration.

Direct-Mail
Campaign

POWERFUL liter-
ature mailed by us
~to your prospects
~over your name.

You pay only a dime
per name for the
entire campaign.

**Shows Results
in Actual Sales!**

Wide Open!

Prospect's Name
Address
City, State

DEALER DEVELOPMENT DOCUMENTS

One of Harley-Davidson's single greatest assets is its small army of authorized dealers, which today number more than 1,400 worldwide. Company founders recognized the value of a strong dealer network from the very beginning. At the time of Harley-Davidson's incorporation in 1907, the United States already had more than forty established motorcycle manufacturers, and a dedicated dealer was often the key to making inroads in a new market. Cultivating a strong—and independently owned—dealer network was one of the best business decisions company founders made.

The earliest dealers were most often super enthusiasts who shared the founders' evangelical excitement for two-wheeled travel. They came from all backgrounds: hardware stores, automobile dealers, even sporting goods outlets. All it took was the right spark of enthusiasm for the product. The Motor Company's first dealer—and for a very long time its most successful dealer—was C. H. Lang, a Chicago-based manufacturer of piano-tuning tools. Lang opened his Harley-Davidson dealership in 1904, three years before company incorporation, as what he hoped would be a profitable sideline. Harley-Davidson only built eight motorcycles in 1905, three of which were sold by Lang. In 1906, Lang sold 24 of the 50 total Harley-Davidsons produced that year; he sold 84

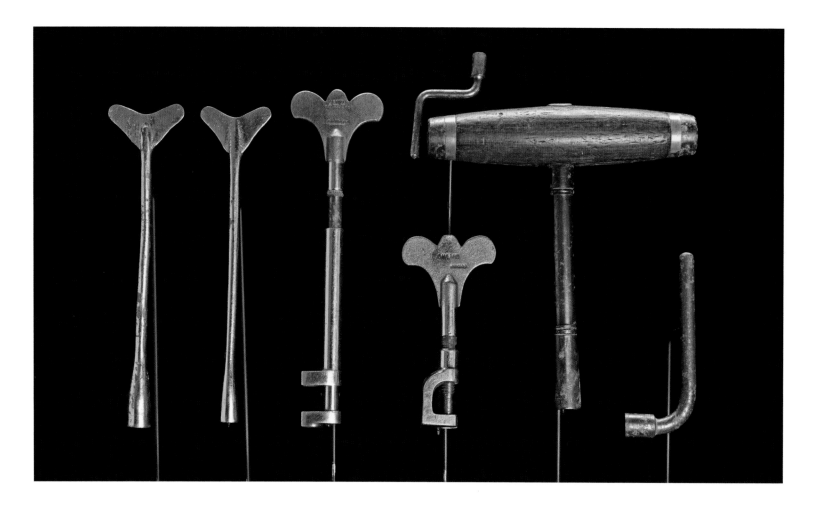

PIANO-TUNING TOOLS MANUFACTURED BY C. H. LANG, ONE OF HARLEY-DAVIDSON'S EARLIEST AND MOST SUCCESSFUL DEALERS.

of 150 in 1907. By 1912, Lang had opened a brand-new dealership on Chicago's Michigan Avenue—the so-called "Miracle Mile"—and his sales volume swelled to a remarkable eight hundred units per year. Piano tuning tools were now officially his sideline.

Dealer development, led by Arthur Davidson, swung into overdrive in 1907. In November of that year, just two months after incorporation, the board of directors voted to rent space at the Chicago Auto Show to recruit dealers, enticing them with a progressive rebate program that awarded price breaks for each additional motorcycle purchased (every fifth bike brought a $30 rebate). Early the next season, Arthur Davidson departed on a tour of the East Coast—riding a Harley-Davidson motorcycle, of course—to personally recruit dealers. A great storyteller with a warm, folksy style, Arthur excelled at this work. By the end of 1908, Harley-Davidson dealerships were established in New York,

800 Harley-Davidsons a Year.

The Harley-Davidson, taken on as a Side Line by a Manufacturer and Dealer in Piano Tuners' Tools, has Resulted in one of the Biggest Selling Successes we Know of.

C. H. LANG

Lang started selling Harley-Davidsons back in 1904, and has gradually increased his business until in 1912 he was selling 800 machines a year. Lang was a motorcycle rider even before he was a Harley-Davidson dealer. His business was the manufacture of piano tuners' tools. He had a small plant and store on East Adams street and it was in these sales rooms that he sold Harley-Davidsons for the first six or seven years.

Finally he outgrew these quarters and opened up one of the finest motorcycle stores I have ever seen, on Michigan avenue, near Seventeenth, where a good store rents for from five to six thousand dollars a year.

One of the first things a person notices in entering Mr. Lang's store is an old Harley-Davidson model. It was one of the first we built and has covered something over 100,000 miles in its ten years of existence. The machine is still in running order and was in daily operation on the streets of Chicago up until a few months ago when Mr. Lang traded the machine in as part payment on a late model.

The story of Mr. Lang's rapid rise in the motorcycle business is too well known to need any comment here. Lang says the Harley-Davidson is responsible for the size of his business but most certainly his own hard work has helped a good deal. Lang, we believe, is the only motorcycle dealer in Chicago who has handled one make for more than two or three years. Mr. Lang has sold the Harley-Davidson for ten and never handled any other.

GASOLINE AND OILS.
A.G. MUELLER,
GARAGE
HARLEY-DAVIDSON MOTOR CYCLES

Chicago, Philadelphia, Atlanta, Newark, and many other major American cities. By 1912, more than two hundred Harley-Davidson dealers had been established across the United States, and the Motor Company sold more than nine thousand motorcycles that year.

By 1916, there were so many Harley-Davidson dealers that Arthur was forced to divide the nation into districts and assign managers to oversee each one. To aid in this effort, the Motor Company produced a variety of materials to entice early dealers and to assist those who had already made a commitment to the brand. The Motor Company also published an internal magazine, *The Harley-Davidson Dealer,* during roughly this same period, which instructed outlets in everything from store layout and marketing fundamentals to advanced repair techniques. A 1916 leaflet declared, "It is our policy to co-operate with Harley-Davidson dealers to the fullest extent in building up a permanent and profitable motorcycle business." Company literature emphasized the importance of a clean, well-lit, and tastefully decorated showroom to "maintain the favorable impression of Harley-Davidson." The company realized even then that attractive and accessible dealerships, operated by well-trained and well-informed specialists, were the difference between mediocre and major sales.

The close-knit company-dealer-customer relationship is one that still defines the Harley-Davidson brand today. It's a relationship founded on loyalty that was hard earned, in all directions. Even in the earliest days, company founders understood the value of maintaining close ties to the customer—and the dealer is effectively the company's first customer. It's a three-way relationship that stood the test of time and defined a shared heritage. Without the existence of such a strong dealer network, Harley-Davidson may well have ended up a footnote to motorcycle history.

BEGINNING OF THE HARLEY-DAVIDSON MUSEUM COLLECTION

8

Although there aren't definite records, evidence suggests that it was sometime around 1915 when Harley-Davidson began systematically assembling the amazing motorcycle collection displayed in the museum today. Legend has it that 1915 was the year when the company began saving at least one motorcycle "right off the line" to represent each production year.

It's thought that, perhaps, this collecting impulse was influenced by Harley-Davidson's participation in the Transportation Palace display at the 1915 Panama-Pacific International Exposition, hosted that year in San Francisco to celebrate the completion of the Panama Canal. Harley-Davidson motorcycles were displayed at the fair alongside models from Indian, Excelsior, and Dayton, and it's suggested that the success of this exhibit, which celebrated the motorcycle as a significant transportation innovation, inspired Motor Company officials to pay closer attention to their mechanical legacy.

At that point, Harley-Davidson started saving at least one example motorcycle from each production year and also began retroactively collecting—or, in some cases, re-creating—example motorcycles from years prior. This "core collection" consists of motorcycles taken directly from the production line or, in some cases, preproduction or engineering test units.

In its earliest days, the collection was housed at Juneau Avenue, but it moved around some in the following years. In the 1950s, it was displayed at the nearby Capitol Drive factory, and then it was relocated to the manufacturing facility in York, Pennsylvania, for a period in the late 1970s, before being returned to Milwaukee. Nowadays, the collection lives in the museum on "The Road," the linear gallery of polished black concrete that extends the length of the building, where more than seventy bikes at a time are arranged three-abreast to form the museum's backbone.

Around five hundred motorcycles are in the archive today, the vast majority of which are completely unrestored, making this one of the most original motorcycle collections in the world. A majority of these bikes show just a handful of miles on the odometer, accumulated just by rolling the bikes back and forth on the archive floor. Items that deteriorate over time—rubber tires or handgrips, for example—are replaced as required, but as a rule of thumb the bikes are only restored as a last resort. After all, a vehicle can only be original once—and you're likely not going to find more original vehicles in any one place than you will at the Harley-Davidson Museum.

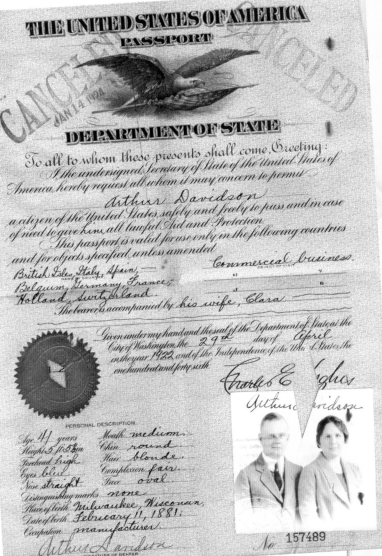

THE UNITED STATES OF AMERICA
PASSPORT
CANCELED *JAN 14 1924*

DEPARTMENT OF STATE

To all to whom these presents shall come, Greeting:
I the undersigned, Secretary of State of the United States of America, hereby request all whom it may concern to permit

Arthur Davidson

a citizen of the United States safely and freely to pass and in case of need to give him all lawful Aid and Protection.

This passport is valid for use only in the following countries and for objects specified, unless amended —

OBJECT OF VISIT — *Commercial business.*

NAME OF COUNTRY — *British Isles, Italy, Spain, Belguim, Germany, France, Holland, Switzerland.*

The bearer is accompanied by his wife, "Clara"

Given under my hand and the seal of the Department of State at the City of Washington, the *29th* day of *April* in the year 1922 and of the Independence of the United States, the one hundred and forty sixth.

Charles E Hughes

PERSONAL DESCRIPTION
Age *41* years
Height *5 ft 5½ in*
Forehead *high*
Eyes *blue*
Nose *straight*
Mouth *medium*
Chin *round*
Hair *blonde*
Complexion *fair*
Face *oval*
Distinguishing marks *none*
Place of birth *Milwaukee, Wisconsin*
Date of birth *February 11, 1881*
Occupation *manufacturer*

Arthur Davidson
SIGNATURE OF BEARER

No. 157489

THE PERSON TO WHOM THIS PASSPORT IS ISSUED HAS DECLARED UNDER OATH, THAT he DESIRES IT FOR USE IN VISITING THE COUNTRIES HEREINAFTER NAMED FOR THE FOLLOWING OBJECTS

Remaining in England & Scotland
(NAME OF COUNTRY) (OBJECT OF VISIT)

in Motor-cycle business
(NAME OF COUNTRY) (OBJECT OF VISIT)

Returning to the United States of America
(NAME OF COUNTRY) (OBJECT OF VISIT)

THIS PASSPORT IS NOT VALID FOR USE IN OTHER COUNTRIES EXCEPT FOR NECESSARY TRANSIT TO OR FROM THE COUNTRIES NAMED.

Good only for *Two* ~~six~~ months from date

Embassy
of the
United States of America.
at
London, England.

To all to whom these presents shall come, Greeting.

I, the undersigned, Ambassador Extraordinary and Plenipotentiary of the United States of America, hereby request all whom it may concern to permit

Arthur Davidson

a Citizen of the United States safely and freely to pass, and in case of need to give him all lawful Aid and Protection.

Description
Age *32* Years
Stature *5* Feet *6* Inches Eng.
Forehead *high*
Eyes *blue*
Nose *regular*
Mouth *medium*
Chin *square*
Hair *fair*
Complexion *fair*
Face *square*

Signature of the Bearer
Arthur Davidson

Given under my hand and the Seal of the Embassy of the United States at London, the *8th* day of *December* in the year 1915 and of the Independence of the United States the one hundred and *39th*.

Walter Hines Page

No. 4646

9

ARTHUR DAVIDSON'S PASSPORTS

Harley-Davidson's early years were characterized by explosive growth, and this rapid expansion was not limited just to the United States of America. The firm was already well established in the US by 1912, with over two hundred authorized dealers selling nine thousand motorcycles per year, and word was rapidly spreading around the world about Harley-Davidson motorcycles. Later that same year, Harley-Davidson established its first international distributorship in Japan, marking the first time Harley-Davidson motorcycles were sold outside US borders.

European sales were established through a London office in 1914—referred to as the "Foreign Branch"—and London soon became the hub for all sales outside of North and South America, playing an enormous role by strengthening positions in numerous European countries, as well as in India, Russia, and South Africa.

Sales Manager Arthur Davidson spearheaded this aggressive international expansion, and the museum collection includes many artifacts that serve as evidence of his extensive international travels—including this early passport revealing details about a 1917 business trip to Australia and New Zealand. Davidson loved to travel abroad, and his wife, Clara, who shared his passion for adventure, often accompanied him on these trips. Company documents reveal that his first foreign trip occurred in 1915, when he traveled to England and Scotland (the latter was his ancestral home). Clara joined Arthur on this 1917 excursion, which included not only stops in Australia and New Zealand but also Tasmania and Pago Pago, the capital of American Samoa.

Note that Davidson's 1917 travel document bears little resemblance to a modern passport booklet. Prior to World War I, a typical American passport document was an oversized, 11 x 17-inch diploma that included a large engraved seal of the US Department of the State at the top (repeated in red wax at the bottom), room for the bearer's description and signature, and ample space for additional data such as "accompanied by his wife," all written in an exaggerated, ornate script. Early travel documents also served double duty as working visas—later passports in the collection list Davidson's purpose for travel as commercial business, or more specifically, "motorcycle business."

By 1920, Harley-Davidson was the largest motorcycle manufacturer in the world, with operating subsidiaries in sixty-seven countries. The Motor Company employed representatives in such far-flung locations as Australia, Holland, South Africa, and Argentina to further expand and support international operations—the collection includes a selection of promotional post-cards used by these agents during the mid-teens to raise awareness of the Harley-Davidson brand. The collection also includes numerous foreign-language marketing brochures from the late '20s, including Japanese, Dutch, Spanish, and Chinese language versions of the 1928 model year catalog—demonstrating just how broad the reach of the Motor Company had become.

This early and aggressive foreign expansion played a key role in the health and prosperity of Harley-Davidson through the '20s, especially when the US market began to constrict in response to both a deep recession and the emergence of cheaper and more practical transportation solutions offered by US auto manufacturers. In many parts of Europe during that same period, demand for Harley-Davidson motorcycles exceeded the number of available vehicles, in stark contrast to the home market where demand was shrinking. During some years in the 1920s, overseas sales made up as much as 75 percent of the amount earned by domestic dealers, in fact.

Harley-Davidson remains a global presence today, and in fact, it is increasing its international footprint. Some of Harley-Davidson's most significant growth in recent years has come from Africa and the Middle East, while continued sales success in India, Asia, and other expanding markets help support the Motor Company's bottom line. Harley-Davidson currently operates assembly facilities in India and Brazil and recently announced construction of an additional assembly facility in Thailand to better serve the Asia-Pacific region. Harley-Davidson might be America's motorcycle company, but the freewheeling American spirit Harley-Davidson represents exerts a powerful influence far beyond American borders—then and now.

¡La Motocicleta S

De Dos Cilindros — 1200 c.c.

No tiene igual como moto sola o con side-car por su gran potencia, velocidad pasmosa y maravillosa facilidad y confort con que camina. Posee todas las famosas características Harley-Davidson: poste de asiento de resorte, tijeras delanteras de resorte y neumáticos balloon.

**De Dos Cilindros — 1200 c.c.
Con Doble Eje de Levas**

El modelo más veloz para uso ordinario que fabrica la Harley-Davidson. El trabajo independiente de las levas regulariza perfectamente los tiempos del motor, aumenta la compresión y da más revoluciones por minuto. — Este es el secreto de su aceleración instantánea, de su vertiginosa velocidad y de su estupenda potencia.

Motocamión Repartidor MXP

Muchos comerciantes están mejorando su servicio de reparto y aumentando sus ventas con el uso de los rápidos y bien construidos Carritos Repartidores Harley-Davidson. Es el vehículo repartidor más económico que se conoce. Reduce en dos terceras partes el costo de reparto por cualquier otro medio automotriz y con este ahorro se compra un motocamión.

EN mañanas estivales, bajo cielo turquí inu aire fresco y puro a la velocidad del viento, a de ricas cosechas — por elegantes Boulevar olas rumorosas del océano se quiebran azotando la escarpadas montañas hasta traspasar las crestas de majestuosa fiera, abriéndose paso por abruptos s pero siempre dominada por la mano que la guía. los quince, los treinta, los cincuenta kilómetros siempre vastos horizontes, multicolores paisajes de alegría, de juventud....! ¡Eso es motociclism

La Harley-Davidson por doquiera es la agrada de millares de entusiastas deportistas. Es com que, al potente vibrar de sus entrañas de ac haciendo de cada minuto un momento de ine motocicleta tan cómoda, tan suave al camina

Por su hermosa apariencia, por su correcto Harley-Davidson goza de popularidad mundi es la Motocicleta Suprema!

HARLEY · DA

Armstrong & Walker Portland 1913

Armstrong & Walker Portland 1913

Tryouts at Portland 1913

10

OTTO WALKER'S SCRAPBOOK

Otto Walker was one of the very first riders signed to the Harley-Davidson Wrecking Crew when the Motor Company "officially" returned to motorcycle racing competition in 1914. More importantly, Walker was the first to win a national race for the company when he took the victory at the Federation of American Motorcyclists' 300-mile road race at Venice, California, on April 4, 1915. Walker went on to become one of the winningest riders of the early Wrecking Crew era, setting numerous speed records during his eight-year professional racing career—including, in 1921, earning the distinction of being the first rider to average more than 100 miles per hour in a race.

Not only was Walker a wizard on the racetrack, it turns out he was a fine documentarian as well—as evidenced by this scrapbook, a one-of-a-kind artifact that collects page after page of photos, news clippings, and other materials documenting Walker's racing exploits circa 1919–1921. Not only does the scrapbook catalog Walker's accomplishments, the contents also present those of his teammates, including Leslie "Red" Parkhurst and Albert "Shrimp" Burns, during some of the Wrecking Crew's most successful years. Walker's scrapbook is a treasure trove of early American motorcycle racing history, detailing the personalities, motorcycles, and racing venues that defined that era—all curated with Walker's uniquely personal touch.

The California-born Walker—nicknamed "Camelback" for his distinctive, arched-back riding style he claimed gave him an aerodynamic advantage—was a hugely successful West Coast amateur when he joined the Wrecking Crew. He turned pro at the start of the 1914 season and almost immediately was injured in a crash that forced him to sit out the rest of that year. Walker returned with a vengeance in 1915, giving Harley-Davidson its first national victory on the streets of Venice, California, defeating all the other major factory teams—still considered an upset win, even though he was riding a factory Harley-Davidson. Walker promptly followed his Venice victory with an even more impressive win in July at the prestigious Dodge City 300. This was the biggest

motorcycle race in America, contested that year by twenty-nine factory entries from six different motorcycle manufacturers. There was no doubt—Walker was the best racer in 1915, and Harley-Davidson was now the motorcycle to beat.

Walker was sidelined for most of the 1916 season when he injured his leg in a crash at Chicago. As soon as he was well enough to walk again, he joined the US Army to serve in World War I (his military ID tags are also displayed at the museum), and he served for two years as an aviation electrician. Promptly upon being discharged, Walker was greeted with a telegram from Harley-Davidson Racing Manager Bill Ottaway—would he consider rejoining the Wrecking Crew at the 1919 Marion (Indiana) road race? Walker replied yes, and he showed up on the starting line at Marion wearing what would soon become his signature item—a German aviator helmet salvaged during his time overseas.

That Labor Day race at Marion unofficially marked the return of motorcycle racing to postwar America. It was a hugely popular event, with more than fifteen thousand fans in attendance— some traveling by motorcycle from as far away as the West Coast. Walker didn't win that day—he finished just behind winner Red Parkhurst, as Harley-Davidson riders swept the top three places. Walker returned to his winning ways in 1920, however, emerging victorious at America's biggest motorcycle races. The first was

the 2-mile championship event held at the legendary Sheepshead Bay board track in Brooklyn, New York, where, in front of a crowd of seventeen thousand people, he completed the 2-mile course in just over a minute, averaging 96 miles per hour. He followed this with a win at the 100-mile national held at Ascot Park in Los Angeles, proving the Motor Company could count on him to deliver at major events.

Walker's biggest moment, however, came on February 2, 1921, at a non-title race in Fresno, California. Here, riding the Harley-Davidson eight-valve V-twin, he became the first racer to win a race at an average speed of more than 100 miles per hour. Harley-Davidson celebrated this achievement roundly, as could be expected, issuing a nationwide "Flashogram" announcing Walker's record-setting performance, with the headline "Oh Boy, Some Clean-Up!" Hoping to further capitalize on this feat, the Motor Company rented the legendary Beverly Hills Speedway in January of 1922 for Walker to attempt to cover 100 miles in an hour. Engine trouble kept him from the ultimate goal, but Walker was still able to break six American speed records for distances ranging from 1 to 50 miles. These feats and more are all contained in Walker's scrapbook—the measure of a truly remarkable career—and it's fair to say that Otto Walker went out on top when he retired from racing at the end of the 1922 season.

11

EIGHT-VALVE RACER

Harley-Davidson's considerable racing success in the teens and early 1920s was not limited to the Wrecking Crew's exploits in America. Harley-Davidson also enjoyed success in other nations, including England, where one of the greatest English motorcycle racers of all time, Freddie Dixon, competed on this exceedingly rare eight-valve race bike. "Flying Freddie" Dixon enjoyed particular success at the Brooklands circuit in Surrey, where in 1923 this bike earned the legendary Gold Star for lapping the treacherous Outer Circuit at more than 100 miles per hour.

Developed by Harley-Davidson Racing Manager Bill Ottaway, with considerable assistance from British-born combustion guru Harry Ricardo, who conceived the revolutionary four-valve cylinder heads, this twin-cam, 61-cubic-inch V-twin boasted a potent 120-mile-per-hour top speed. Not only was it spectacularly fast, the eight-valve racer was also spectacularly expensive at $1,500—compared to $350 for competitor Indian's eight-valve racer. Some suspect that Harley-Davidson priced the eight-valve racers "not to sell" on purpose to prevent privateer racers from upstaging the factory team. Perhaps for similar reasons, the eight-valve racers were produced in extremely limited numbers. Official production figures don't exist, but it's widely believed that fewer than twenty eight-valve racers were ever built.

Harley-Davidson Winnings Open the Season

HARLEY-DAVIDSON speed is the result of scientifically correct design, good workmanship, and high-grade materials.

At Goulburn, Australia, April 24th, the Harley-Davidson won the Canberra Club's 50-mile road race.

At Mortlake, Australia, April 24th, the Harley-Davidson secured the fastest circuit trophy in the Victorian Club's road race, covering the 102 miles in 97 minutes.

At Fort Worth, Texas, April 23rd, the Harley-Davidson ridden by Sam Correnti, won every race on the program and broke the track record by 2 4-5 seconds.

At Roanoke, Virginia, April 24th, Ray Weishaar, riding a single-cylinder Harley-Davidson, won three of the four races on the program, and was leading by a half lap at 8 miles when he blew a tire in the 15-mile open event. In the 10-mile open the Harley-Davidson took first and second, lapping all competitors, including a special four-valve single and a ported single of other make. In the 1-mile open event the Harley-Davidson broke the state record.

Harley-Davidson Motor Co., *Milwaukee, Wis., U. S. A.*
Producers of High-Grade Motorcycles for More Than Fourteen Years

LEGENDARY BRITISH RACER F. W. "FLYING FREDDIE" DIXON, POSING IN 1923 ON HIS EIGHT-VALVE RACER, NOW PART OF THE MUSEUM COLLECTION.

Not surprisingly, eight-valve Harley-Davidson motorcycles won every single US national championship race in 1921, cementing the Wrecking Crew's unbeatable reputation. What was surprising was Harley-Davidson's decision to exit racing the next year, in response to downward economic pressure and a difficult business environment that could no longer support the racing program's substantial costs. It's believed that most of the original eight-valve racers were destroyed that year; precious few like this one were exported to other countries, where they could continue their winning ways.

The ex–Freddie Dixon racer, the first motorcycle that greets visitors upon entering the museum's competition gallery, is thought to be one of just three eight-valve racers that still exist today. After Dixon transitioned from racing motorcycles to racing cars in 1928, his eight-valve was returned to the United States, where it eventually ended up in the collection of John "J. D." Cameron—notorious as a co-founder of the Los Angeles–based

Boozefighters MC, the group that allegedly inspired the classic Marlon Brando biker film *The Wild One*. For the duration of Cameron's ownership, the bike remained as-configured by Dixon for road racing, complete with a two-speed transmission, clutch, and brakes—all of which were considered optional in the period, as the original eight-valves were built for board-track racing.

A subsequent owner returned the bike to something that more closely represents what is believed to be its original board-track configuration—a decision that Cameron criticized until his final days, staunchly believing that the Dixon version of this bike was the most historically significant version. You can see how restoring a motorcycle can sometimes be controversial, especially when it's a race bike with such a rich—and relatively undocumented—history. The bike remains today restored in its board-track configuration, museum officials having decided that the more-original version was a better representative for the archive collection.

The Harley-Davidson Enthusiast

ALRIGHT, STENO! I'M FINISHED WITH 'EM-! DRAW THE CURTAINS SLOWLY AND LET THE FOLKS SEE OUR HOMOGENEOUS CONGLOMERATION OF HORSEPOWER IRONS!

DARK GLASSES TO PREVENT EYE-STRAIN FROM GLARE OF NEW MODELS

PRIVATE!

KEEP OUT!

"UNK" FRANK

The NEW 1930 MODELS NOT TO BE OPENED TILL NOW!

Uncle Frank's Service Dope

By Uncle Frank Himself

Hark! Hark! New policy in force! Say, you fellers are swamping your old Uncle. I'm getting so many, many letters that I can't begin to answer them all. I know that some of you boys wonder why Uncle Frank does not answer your questions right away. Well, the reason is that

The Schebler carburetor as used on 1928-29-30 Harley-Davidsons can be made to operate with a lean mixture. But you should not cut the gas down too much for if you do, you will cause overheating of the motor and will not obtain the power there is in the motor. It is not good economy point

Nobby Ned

TO BE SURE OF GOOD "BREAKS" GET A HARLEY-DAVIDSON-1928!

(1) I'M SORRY YOU ARE 'WAY BACK ON THE RUMBLE SEAT, DORIS, AND CAN'T JOIN OUR CONVERSATION! — OH-THAT'S ALL RIGHT-ILL SEND YOU A POSTCARD

(2) DAM THOSE BRAKES! X!!!-!!! CRASH! BANG! CRINKLE! CRUNK

(3) NOW-I GOTTA GIT OUT AND GIT UNDER-ITS THOSE BRAKES AGAIN! — SAY-WHAT YOU RUN INTO ME FOR-IM NOT A SPEAK-EASY!

(4) WHY, HELLO NED-HOW DID YOU STOP BESIDE ME SO QUICKLY? — IT'S MY NEW HARLEY-DAVIDSON "FORE" WHEEL BRAKE-DORIS-ALWAYS STOPS AT THE RIGHT PLACE!

(5) NED-WHAT HAS HAPPENED TO YOUR SIDE CAR-IT'S AWFULLY CHUMMY! — IT'S THE 1928 HARLEY-DAVIDSON -BUILT-TO PROMOTE FRIENDSHIP! DAM THESE BRAKES!

(6) THIS NEW 1928 BRAKE MAKES LIFE A PLEASURE! — IT SURE GAVE YOU A GOOD "BREAK" DIDN'T IT NED?

12

THE ENTHUSIAST ISSUE #1

Harley-Davidson's founders understood the value of a good story. Mythmaking was a big part of the Motor Company's early marketing efforts, and to aid these efforts, Harley-Davidson created a variety of publications to communicate directly with dealers and consumers both. Titles included *The Harley-Davidson Dealer*, launched in 1912, followed by a consumer-focused magazine, *The Enthusiast*, in 1916. "See that your riders get *The Enthusiast* and they'll read it," a period dealer communication suggested. "Few things do more to maintain the enthusiasm of the rider for the sport than this little magazine."

The earliest issues of *The Enthusiast* were largely composed of reader-submitted stories and photographs, supplemented with "helpful and entertaining" articles generated by moonlighting Motor Company employees writing under pseudonyms—for reasons that aren't entirely clear, there was a policy in the early days of not identifying *The Enthusiast* staff. The characters they created—Nobby Ned, Hap Hayes, Vic Valve, and many more—soon became some of the most well-known and popular personalities in the motorcycle industry, despite the fact they didn't exist.

Many of the most popular characters were created by Hap Jameson, who became the voice of Harley-Davidson during the 1920s. And his most popular character, far and away, was the one he named Uncle Frank. Uncle Frank was best known for expert mechanical advice, though he also wrote short fiction and reviewed Harley-Davidson's new models too. Frank was everybody's favorite uncle, so popular that *Enthusiast* readers would regularly knock on the Juneau factory's front door and demand to meet Frank, only to shuffle off disappointed when told that he wasn't real. Hap Jameson was a very real person, however, and an awful lot of Jameson's real personality was woven into the character of Uncle Frank.

A successful amateur racer in his youth, Jameson got his start in business in 1910, working as a sales agent for C. H. Lang. By 1912, Jameson was officially working at Harley-Davidson, beginning as a test rider before moving to the service department. Jameson had a gift for conversation and truly loved to help people, skills that served him well during his next position as district sales manager in the Pacific Northwest. After this, he wrote service manuals and instructed at the Service School, before he was finally moved to the advertising department, taking over as publicity director. His new duties there included managing *The Enthusiast* magazine.

Jameson's arrival in 1922 marked the beginning of an enormously entertaining run for *The Enthusiast*. First came the aptly named "Just for Fun" column, followed soon after with the last-page "Nobby Ned" comic strip. Uncle Frank appeared later that year, introduced as follows: "My name is Frank and I'm going to tell you some interesting and money-saving information, each month, about your motorcycle. I'll make 'em short and snappy—that's the way you want 'em, isn't it?"

Even without naming names, it was clear that Jameson was composing the bulk of the magazine—his writing style was that distinctive. The tone of *The Enthusiast* was very playful, mischievous even. Uncle Frank wasn't afraid to wax philosophic about "moonshine" or "homebrew," for example, even during the depths of Prohibition, and he was never too shy to engage in flirtatious behavior with his lovely assistant, Steno (short for stenographer). Uncle Frank once even offered child-rearing advice—"Mix his spinach with gasoline, and he must cut his teeth on piston rings." Anonymity, it seemed, was liberating.

Uncle Frank wasn't always frivolous. He was quick with a joke, sure, but his technical advice was always trustworthy and he never failed to promote Harley-Davidson's product line. Especially in the 1920s, when Harley-Davidson's product could be considered outdated against more modern designs from other manufacturers, Harley-Davidson was still the more desirable brand. Much of this popularity could be traced directly to the camaraderie and community cultivated by Jameson in the pages of *The Enthusiast*.

Uncle Frank departed *The Enthusiast* in August 1931, when Jameson took a new position at Harley-Davidson acting as a liaison to the American Motorcyclist Association. *The Enthusiast* carried on without him, maybe a slightly less entertaining but no less vital compendium of the Harley-Davidson experience. At the museum, you'll see references to—if not actual examples of—*The Enthusiast* surface over and over again. It seems to be the one constant, the magazine of record for the American motorcycle industry. *The Enthusiast* still survives today, though it's published under the name *HOG*—subtitled "For the Harley-Davidson Enthusiast since 1916"—making it one of the longest continuously published motorcycle magazines in the world.

Hap Jameson piloting a sidecar rig in 1925. Perhaps that's his lovely assistant "Steno" riding in the sidehack?

SEAL OF THE CITY OF WILMINGTON
DELAWARE

CITY OF WILMINGTON
DELAWARE

GEORGE BLACK
SUPERINTENDENT OF PUBLIC SAFETY

DEPARTMENT OF PUBLIC SAFETY
BUREAU OF POLICE

July 5, 1929.

To whom it may concern:-

    This is to certify that Miss Vivian Bales who is on a Motorcycle Tour from Albany, Ga., to Milwaukee, Wisconsin, stopped in my office on the above date.

    Any courtesies that you may be able to extend to Miss Bales will certainly be appreciated by me.

Very truly yours,

George Black

Superintendent of Public Safety.

&

Secretary of

International Asso.Chiefs of Police.

13

VIVIAN BALES' SCRAPBOOK

Women make up more than 50 percent of the population, but according to the most recent Motorcycle Industry Council study (2015), only 14 percent of all motorcycle owners in America are female. Remarkably, though, more than 60 percent of those women riders choose Harley-Davidson motorcycles. Some of this success is no doubt due to recent efforts by Harley-Davidson to make the sport more appealing to women, frequently featuring female riders in advertising, designing and building smaller and easier-to-handle motorcycles, and creating events and programming just for women.

But this isn't just a modern phenomenon. Women have been a vibrant part of Harley-Davidson culture from the very beginning, and early pioneers such as Vivian Bales and other historic female Harley-Davidson riders have been inspiring women to ride for more than one hundred years.

Bales's scrapbook, on display at the museum alongside numerous other historical artifacts (including her American Motorcyclist Association long-distance award pin and stacks of fan mail from as far away as South Africa and Japan), reveals just how well-known—and how widely known—Miss Bales was in the 1930s. Nicknamed "The Enthusiast Girl" due to the frequency of her appearances on the pages of Harley-Davidson's corporate magazine *The Enthusiast*, Bales's two-wheeled escapades first attracted the attention of company officials in 1929. That was when she rode her motorcycle from her home in Albany, Georgia, to Harley-Davidson headquarters in Milwaukee and beyond, returning home after three months and nearly 5,000 miles covered.

Bales—a 5-foot 2-inch, 95-pound dance teacher—was already a seasoned adventurer by that time, having tested herself with many shorter trips around the southeastern United States—often accompanied by her best friend, Josephine Johnson, riding on the passenger seat. Bales taught herself to ride at age seventeen in 1926, when she purchased her first Harley-Davidson, and she often had to sneak out of the house to ride. "I always wanted to do something that most girls wouldn't do," Bales said shortly after her 1929 adventure, "and my motorcycle gave me the chance to satisfy my adventurous spirit."

Other early female motorcycle pioneers are celebrated in the museum collection, including Della Crewe, who covered 5,378 miles circling America in 1915 with only her scruffy terrier named Trouble riding in the sidecar. Crewe's incredible journey over terrible roads took her from Waco, Texas—her hometown—to New York City to Milwaukee and then back to Texas, with a detour to Florida too. Later in her riding career, Crewe adventured even farther abroad, to Central and South America (she was arrested in Panama for riding without a motorcycle license) and even the island nation of Cuba.

Bessie Stringfield, the first African-American woman to ride across the United States alone, is also featured at the museum.

The adopted daughter of a wealthy Irish ex-pat who always encouraged Bessie to chase her dreams, Stringfield got her first motorcycle—a 1928 Indian Scout—at age sixteen. Except for that first bike, Stringfield was a dyed-in-the-wool Harley-Davidson loyalist, owning twenty-seven Milwaukee-made motorcycles over the next sixty-six years. That inaugural cross-country expedition in the 1930 was the first of many for the so-called "Motorcycle Queen of Miami," who eventually rode through all forty-eight contiguous states, plus Mexico, Canada, and Hawaii.

Stringfield was famous for what she called her "money method" of trip planning, where she would toss a penny onto a map and ride to wherever the penny landed. Decades before the Civil Rights Movement took hold, Stringfield was frequently forced to sleep outside after being turned away from hotels or motels because of her race. Later, during World War II, Stringfield volunteered for a domestic motorcycle dispatch position, and she was the only woman in the unit traveling over rough roads to deliver classified documents. She also raced flat track and even performed with a carnival motordrome show—there wasn't much on two wheels that Bessie Stringfield couldn't and didn't do.

Of course, there's no way the museum's appreciation of female motorcycling pioneers would be complete without highlighting the tale of Avis and Effie Hotchkiss, the mother-daughter duo who in 1915 gained notoriety for riding from Brooklyn to San

Harley~Davidson Motor Co

MOTORCYCLES SIDECARS **HARLEY-DAVIDSON** AND PACKAGE TRUCKS

WALTER DAVIDSON, PRES. AND GENL. MGR.
WM. A. DAVIDSON, VICE PRES. AND WORKS MGR.
WM. S. HARLEY, TREASURER AND CHIEF ENGINEER
ARTHUR DAVIDSON, SEC'Y. AND GENL. SALES MGR.

CABLE ADDRESS "HARDAVMOC"
CODES LIEBERS WESTERN UNI
A.B.C. 4TH & 5TH EDITION
BENTLEY'S AND
A.B.C. 5TH IMPROVED.

Milwaukee, Wis., U.S.A.

IN REPLY REFER TO DESK E-3   May 16, 1929

TO HARLEY-DAVIDSON DEALERS
WHOM IT MAY CONCERN:

     It seems a bit ridiculous to have to introduce
the bearer of this letter, for Miss Vivian Bales of Albany,
Georgia, riding as the Harley-Davidson Enthusiast Girl is
known to Harley-Davidson friends the world over.

     Miss Bales has undertaken a rather ambitious
program, however, one which is in keeping with her pluck.
She has planned this trip to the Harley-Davidson factory
over a course which contacts many Harley-Davidson dealers.
This enterprise is backed entirely by Miss Bales, having
no financial assistance or aid other than obtained through
her own resources. After reaching the Harley-Davidson factory, Miss Bales will write a story of her journey for
Harley-Davidson Enthusiast publication.

     As Editor of the Enthusiast, I am personally in-
terested in seeing Miss Bales' journey a pleasant and successful one. Therefore, it is my wish that you as a Harley-
Davidson dealer extend her every courtesy and aid her in
any way which will assist in the completion of this journey,
especially you should see to it that her "45" model Harley-
Davidson is in nice purring condition and always topped off
with Genuine Harley-Davidson Oil, not forgetting the gas
tank. In case that Miss Bales needs financial assistance,
then this introductory letter should be sufficient for you
to aid her in this respect, for this order over my signature
is sufficient for reimbursement according to your demands.

     All of us should work together in putting over
this wonderful exhibition of motorcycling and I feel certain
that those who read this introduction will agree with me and
will help to carry it out to the letter.

       Yours sincerely,

Enthusiast Editor   H.E. Hap Jameson
HEJ:MP   HARLEY-DAVIDSON MOTOR CO.

60 Peachtree St
Atlanta, Ga

Miss Vivian Bales
Albany
Ga

Francisco. Effie piloted the bike while
Avis rode in a sidecar. Always a tomboy,
Effie was taught to ride (and repair) her
motorcycle by her brother, Everett, when
she was just sixteen years old. After just
two days of instruction, she bought her
first motorcycle, and four years later, on
May 2, 1915, she and her mother set out
from Brooklyn to cross the country by
motorcycle. "Fear doesn't bother me," Avis
said just before their departure. "I can
safely trust my daughter. . . . I do not fear
breakdowns for Effie, being a most careful
driver, is a good mechanic and does her
own repairing with her own tools."

It took Effie and Avis two months to
complete their 9,000-mile journey, and they
never once had to deploy the revolver
they packed along for safety—though at one
point Effie did have to fashion an inner
tube from a discarded rain poncho and
later replace the sidecar wheel with one
borrowed from a farm threshing machine.
Effie proved a careful driver and fine
mechanic, indeed.

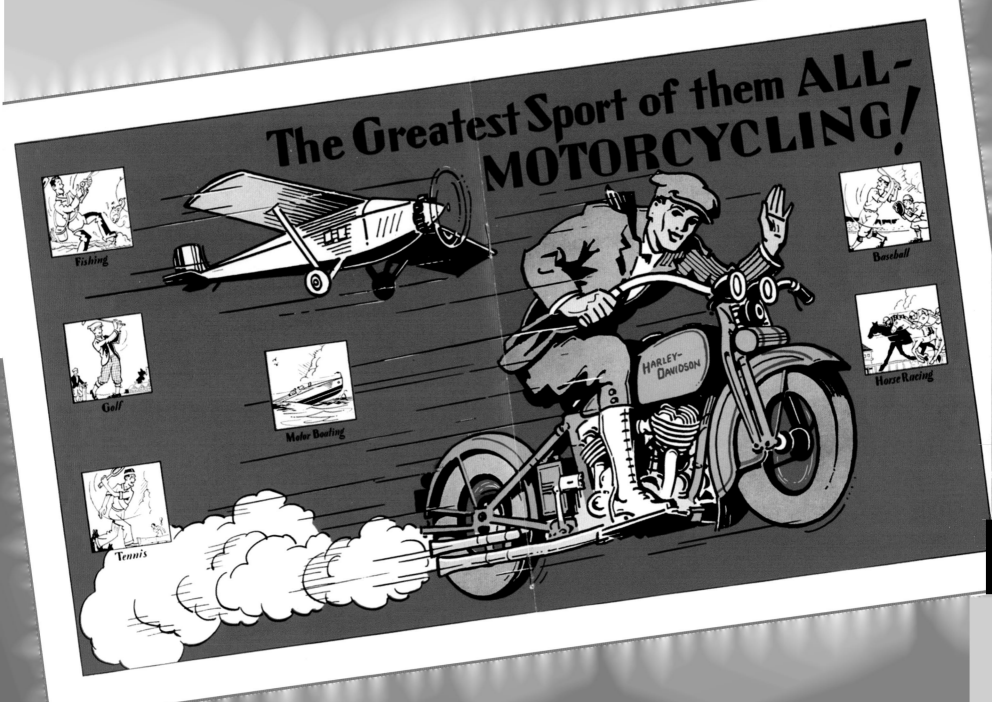

14

THE BEGINNING OF LIFESTYLE MARKETING

Much of the early success of motorcycles in America was driven purely by economics. In the earliest days of motorized transportation, two-wheeled vehicles were cheaper to buy, cheaper to operate, and easier to maintain than four-wheeled vehicles, and so they were much more popular. Any economic advantage had all but evaporated by 1925, however. Production efficiencies and economies of scale had greatly improved, and that year, for the first time ever, Harley-Davidson's big twin motorcycles cost $5 more than Henry Ford's universal Model T automobile.

Company President Walter Davidson summed up the challenge in this statement from 1926: "Way back in 1905, the single cylinder motorcycle was used partly as a sporting proposition and also very largely as economical transportation. The automobile was high-price, the cheapest car being in the neighborhood of $1,000, whereas your motorcycle sold in the neighborhood of $200." Now that cars were cheaper than motorcycles, however, Harley-Davidson's long-running claim of "economical, reliable family transportation" was no longer as credible to consumers as it was before.

This economic shift impacted the motorcycle industry in many serious ways, starting with a rapid decline in sales. Harley-Davidson was the largest motorcycle company in the world in

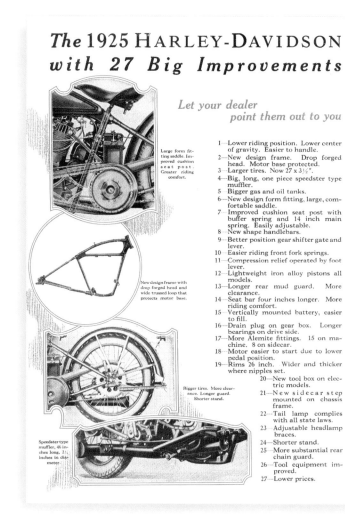

1920, but the automobile's growing popularity posed a serious threat to the Motor Company's bottom line. American motorcycle registrations peaked that same year, and then began to decline at the precipitous rate of ten thousand to fifteen thousand per year for the next few seasons. This industry-wide recession caused Harley-Davidson to post its first loss in 1921—revenue dropped that year by 50 percent, which amounted to $6.5 million—followed by another losing year in 1924.

Consumers were switching to four wheels at an alarming pace, and Harley-Davidson needed to seriously rethink it way it built—and the way that it marketed—its motorcycle products. Appearance and style quickly became as important as utility and price.

As the pure novelty of motorized transportation faded, consumers began to pay more and more attention to subjective factors like design and style. As motorcycles became less utilitarian and more

THE 1925 JDCB MODEL WAS ONE
OF THE FIRST HARLEY-DAVIDSONS
DESIGNED AND MARKETED ON THE
BASIS OF STYLE AND PERFORMANCE.

recreational in nature, product attributes such as looks, luxury, and sporting performance became increasingly more important to Harley-Davidson engineers and designers—and more important to the advertising department too. Harley-Davidson reacted to evolving consumer tastes not only by designing new and more fashionable products, but also by altering its marketing message to better connect with the emergent recreational consumers. This marks the beginning of what we now recognize as the lifestyle marketing of Harley-Davidson motorcycles.

By the mid-1920s, style began driving sales and Harley-Davidson began trumpeting annual design changes in hopes of convincing consumers to trade up to a newer model. The stylishly redesigned 1925 JDCB model was one of the first models designed and marketed with style and performance foremost in mind, and as such it marks a major turning point in Motor Company history. "Isn't this Harley-Davidson a beauty?" the original 1925 advertisement read. "Look at its racy, low sweeping lines. Gee, but won't they stop and look when you come riding down the pike."

The world was changing in the 1920s, sometimes at a dizzying pace. Women got the vote, and movies got sound. Wages rose, and workdays shrank. Consumers had more money and more leisure time available to spend on recreational activities. Motorcycling changed radically in the mid-1920s too. A rapidly expanding US highway system made it easier to ride farther and faster, putting more emphasis on speed and performance.

A new, lower frame that debuted on the 1925 JDCB allowed significantly better handling, while a revised seat and handlebars promised increased rider comfort. This was also the first Harley-Davidson to advertise "streamlined" styling, which was shorthand for a more modern design influence inspired by airplanes and other vehicles specifically designed for top speed. Americans were becoming obsessed with speed and technology, and the soon-to-be-signature teardrop fuel tank, which debuted with this bike, telegraphed Harley-Davidson's newfound commitment to this modern, streamlined design.

By the 1930s, Harley-Davidson's advertising had evolved far beyond the confines of dependable, utilitarian transportation. The Motor Company revamped its entire product line and changed its advertising tactics to remain competitive in this new market, and the commitment to sophisticated design kept sales moving even through the Great Depression. The 1930s rider demanded "a motorcycle of distinction and individuality," a machine that would "stand out and attract attention like a beautiful girl on a windy corner in springtime," ads of the time reported, with nary a mention of economy or reliability. Fun, adventure, and showing off were the new order of the day. In the world of motorcycling, not much has changed since.

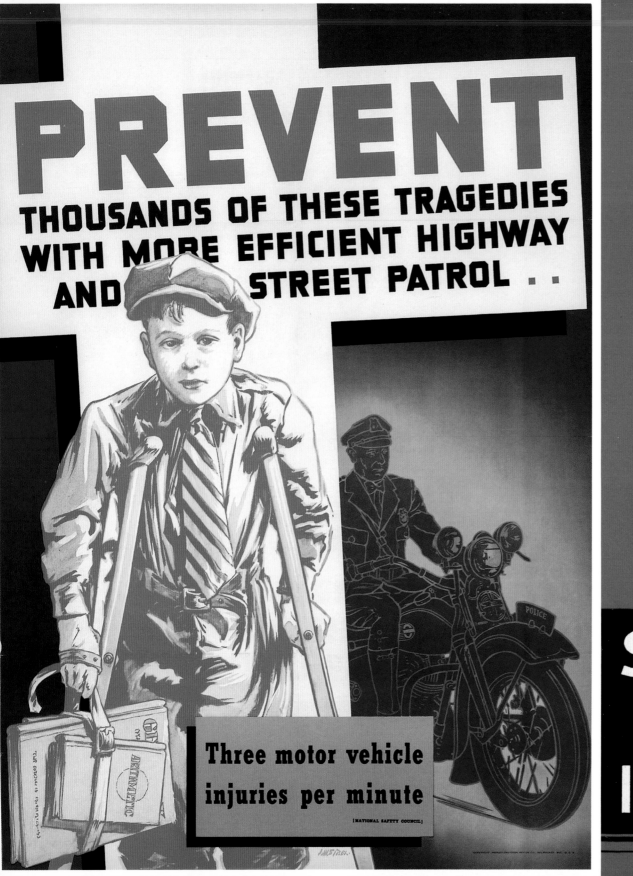

PREVENT

THOUSANDS OF THESE TRAGEDIES WITH MORE EFFICIENT HIGHWAY AND STREET PATROL ...

POLICE

Three motor vehicle injuries per minute

[NATIONAL SAFETY COUNCIL]

The
SLAUGHTER OF THE INNOCENTS

15

PUBLIC SAFETY POSTERS

It's one of the most striking exhibits in the Harley-Davidson Museum, a wall filled with boldly colored posters, all covered with lurid, almost hysterical headlines such as "The Slaughter of the Innocents!" and "Death Takes the Wheel!" The line-drawn imagery is every bit as arresting: a raised broadsword; a grim-reaper skeleton; a silhouetted gangster clutching a pistol; a boy on crutches; a forlorn mother, clutching her injured child. Who—or what—could this horrible enemy be? Warring armies? Organized crime? Zombies?

The answer was none of the above. The enemy was the automobile—or, more specifically, recklessly driven automobiles—and the best way to curb the threat of vehicular violence, at least according to the National Safety Council, the group that produced most of these posters, was to radically increase the number of motorcycle-mounted traffic patrols. Highway deaths were nearing epidemic proportions by the late 1920s, with more and faster vehicles on ever more crowded roads, and little attention paid to safety or driver training. How bad was it? So-called "speed mania" killed more than twenty-seven thousand Americans in 1928 alone. The number of accidents, especially those involving pedestrians and children, rose to unprecedented proportions, inspiring these fear-mongering advertising crusades to advocate for increased police presence in an attempt to reduce this danger.

"Prevent thousands of these tragedies with more efficient highway and street patrol," one poster reads. "The only cure for our deplorable traffic conditions: Adequate street and highway patrol will curb this slaughter," reads another.

Harley-Davidson was quick to respond to this call, especially during the Great Depression. The Motor Company was concerned with public safety, of course, but it was also a good business decision to expand into law enforcement sales and service. Especially in times of downward economic pressure when consumer sales were harder and harder to come by, sales to law enforcement agencies were a steady source of profit that helped the Motor Company weather many economic hard times.

Fast and agile motorcycles offer obvious advantages for pursuit, and so police departments had been replacing horses with motorcycles since the industry began. Harley-Davidson sold its first motorcycle for police use in 1908, and by 1920, more than nine hundred police departments nationwide owned Harley-Davidson motorcycles. By 1925, that number rose dramatically to 2,500 local police and sheriff's departments riding Harley-Davidson bikes. Municipal contracts proved so lucrative that Harley-Davidson even began building special motorcycles for use by fire departments, promoting sidecar rigs as faster and more efficient than oversized fire trucks—especially for fighting smaller household fires.

Police use focused mostly on traffic enforcement, with occasional deployment for ceremonial, escort, and parade duties. As the motorcycle-mounted police officer became a more and more familiar and popular figure, Harley-Davidson's association with law enforcement paid dividends toward its public image as well and was even used to promote sales. One advertisement from 1928 read: "Day after day the Mounted Officer rides his beat—a tireless warning to criminal and traffic law violators. Few are so foolhardy as to ignore his presence—his mere appearance on street and highway compels obedience to the law."

Over the years, Harley-Davidson police motorcycles played a role in some of our nation's most famous—and infamous—moments. Photography displayed in the museum collection showcases a Harley-Davidson-led motorcade escorting President Franklin Delano Roosevelt's funeral cortege in front of the nation's capital in April 1945. When Martin Luther King Jr. led a crowd of civil rights demonstrators through downtown Montgomery, Alabama, in March of 1968, Harley-Davidson Servi-Cars cleared his path. When the Apollo 11 astronauts Buzz Aldrin, Michael Collins, and Neil Armstrong received a ticker-tape parade in New York following their famed lunar mission in 1969, Harley-Davidson police vehicles kept the peace there too.

Harley-Davidson remains a major law enforcement supporter today. Though police sales have faced serious challenges from foreign competitors since the 1970s, dedicated police models and a renewed focused on service and training—including publishing a magazine just for police departments, called *The Mounted Officer*—have helped Harley-Davidson regain a huge portion of the lucrative law enforcement market. Today, Harley-Davidson motorcycles are used by more than three thousand law enforcement agencies in the United States, Canada, and forty-five other countries around the world.

And of course, increases in traffic enforcement and traffic safety have made it so that the average American citizen is half as likely to die in a road accident today than in 1928, which might explain why we're no longer subjected to such sensational safety campaigns as those on display in the Harley-Davidson Museum.

HE PATROLS
FOR YOUR
SAFETY

The
MOUNTED OFFICER'S HAND BOOK

HARLEY-DAVIDSON
POLICE MOTORCYCLES
FOR 1931

19
29
30
31
32
33

FIVE STANDARD
COLOR
COMBINATIONS

LOWEST PRICES
IN HISTORY

EASY TO USE TRANSFERS

RE-ENAMEL THAT OLD
MODEL

STRIPING COLORS

DON'T NEGLECT YOUR
CYLINDERS

VARNISH IS IMPORTANT

HARLEY-
DAVIDSON

HARLEY-
DAVIDSON
TRANSPARENT COPAL
HARLEY-DAVIDSON MOTOR CO.

16

ANY COLOR YOU WANT

Henry Ford, describing his first Model T automobile, once famously remarked to his sales staff that "any customer can have a car painted any color that he wants so long that it is black." It was the same situation with early Harley-Davidson motorcycles, which were first available only in black, and then only in gray, before switching to military olive drab green in 1917 to recognize the Motor Company's support of the US Army during World War I. Style and individuality mattered very little in the early days of motorcycle transportation. Just getting there was good enough; few gave any thought to what they looked like along the way.

Things had changed by the mid-1920s, however. Once cars became cheaper than motorcycles and motorcycles became less valued for practical utility and more important as recreational vehicles, attributes such as performance and style became increasingly more important to buyers. Still, despite its streamlined styling and technical innovation, Harley-Davidson's revolutionary 1925 JDCB model was available in one color and one color only—the same familiar olive drab color seen on every Harley-Davidson made since 1917.

When Arthur Davidson traveled to New York City in early 1927 to attend the annual New York motorcycle show, he brought with him fuel tanks finished in maroon, light green, police blue, and light blue colors. Riders, Davidson finally realized, wanted more vibrant color choices than just olive drab. Not only would more and better color choices give new buyers a reason to consider Harley-Davidson, it would also give current owners a reason to upgrade to a new bike. Olive green remained the Harley-Davidson standard until 1932, but by that time, optional colors and combinations were also offered to "those who wanted something with snap and eye-appeal" for an additional charge. Ordering your motorcycle in Vermillion Red with Black tank panels, for example, added $5.50 to the cost of the bike.

Harley-Davidson accented these new colors with intricate pinstriping and badge art that further differentiated its premium products, creating iconic designs that are still influential even today. These brushes from the museum collection belonged to master painter John Jung, one of the skilled and steady-handed artists who hand-applied these intricate designs to Harley-Davidson motorcycles beginning in the early 1930s. It might seem counter-intuitive that Harley-Davidson was investing in high-end, hand-applied paintwork during the depths of the Great Depression, but with little available funding for new model development, styling was one of the most cost-effective ways to create consumer interest.

The year 1933 was one of the darkest in Harley-Davidson's history. Sagging sales forced the Motor Company to cut prices, and it couldn't afford to develop new models. Instead, Harley-Davidson began offering a choice of standard two-tone color combinations, which, when combined with hand-painted pinstriping and art deco–inspired tank logos, created some striking new looks. The approach worked and Harley-Davidson sold eleven thousand motorcycles in 1934—a 300-percent increase. This was the beginning of Harley-Davidson's long-standing tradition of developing new tank logos to accompany each year's changing paint schemes, which has since become a trademark of Harley-Davidson style.

One of the most fascinating areas of the Harley-Davidson Museum is the "Tank Wall" gallery that stretches the length of the hallway connecting the museum to the archives. That space features one hundred iconic fuel tanks from over the past century, each with its own unique color scheme and logo—a testament to the creativity and style that has long characterized Harley-Davidson designs.

Premium paint is one of the primary selling features on a modern Harley-Davidson motorcycle, and limited-edition custom paint options and color-matching possibilities continue to offer riders endless opportunities to personalize their motorcycle to suit their unique taste and style. Pinstripes, flames, pearl, denim, candy and metallic, silk-screened patterns, decals, emblems, even gold leaf have graced that teardrop tank over the years, showing no limit to the creativity of Harley-Davidson's design staff, or the desire of customers to stand out.

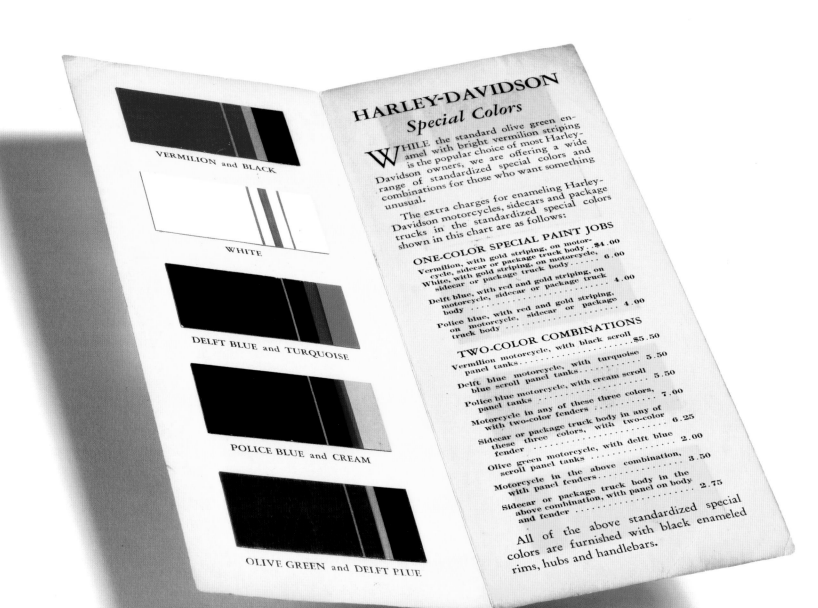

The brochure shown reads:

VERMILION and BLACK

WHITE

DELFT BLUE and TURQUOISE

POLICE BLUE and CREAM

OLIVE GREEN and DELFT BLUE

HARLEY-DAVIDSON
Special Colors

WHILE the standard olive green enamel with bright vermilion striping is the popular choice of most Harley-Davidson owners, we are offering a wide range of standardized special colors and combinations for those who want something unusual.

The extra charges for enameling Harley-Davidson motorcycles, sidecars and package trucks in the standardized special colors shown in this chart are as follows:

ONE-COLOR SPECIAL PAINT JOBS

Vermilion, with gold striping, on motor-cycle, sidecar or package truck body . . $4.00

White, with gold striping, on motorcycle, sidecar or package truck body 6.00

Delft blue, with red and gold striping, on motorcycle, sidecar or package truck body 4.00

Police blue, with red and gold striping, on motorcycle, sidecar or package truck body 4.00

TWO-COLOR COMBINATIONS

Vermilion motorcycle, with black scroll panel tanks $5.50

Delft blue motorcycle, with turquoise blue scroll panel tanks 5.50

Police blue motorcycle, with cream scroll panel tanks 5.50

Motorcycle in any of these three colors, with two-color fenders 7.00

Sidecar or package truck body in any of these three colors, with two-color fender 6.25

Olive green motorcycle, with delft blue scroll panel tanks 2.00

Motorcycle in the above combination, with panel fenders 3.50

Sidecar or package truck body in the above combination, with panel on body and fender 2.75

All of the above standardized special colors are furnished with black enameled rims, hubs and handlebars.

17

THE KNUCKLEHEAD

The year was 1935 and the mood was still mostly grim inside the American motorcycle industry. Five years of economic stagnation caused by the Great Depression had gutted the motorcycle business. Harley-Davidson saw sales plunge from a high of 24,000 bikes in 1929 to just 3,700 in 1933. The situation was so bad that Harley-Davidson hadn't even bothered to host a dealer convention since 1929—with little to talk about beyond new color options for the same stale Flathead lineup, what was the point?

But 1935 felt different. Economic indicators were just beginning to trend upward, and analysts could see the faintest light at the end of the long, dark economic tunnel. And there were rumors from Milwaukee—a few sightings, even—of a new motorcycle said to be so revolutionary that it might lift Harley-Davidson out of the doldrums. So when the Motor Company announced its first dealer convention in five years, slated for November of 1935, stakeholders had reason to get excited.

Dealers traveled from as far away as Japan to gather in the grand ballroom of Milwaukee's Schroeder Hotel, where they watched with rapt attention as Chief Engineer William S. Harley pulled the sheet to reveal the breathtaking 1936 Harley-Davidson EL. The design was magnificent, a perfect art deco evolution of the old streamlined shape that looked like nothing more than the future. At the center of it all was an all-new and thoroughly modern V-twin engine, complete with overhead valves, hemispherical

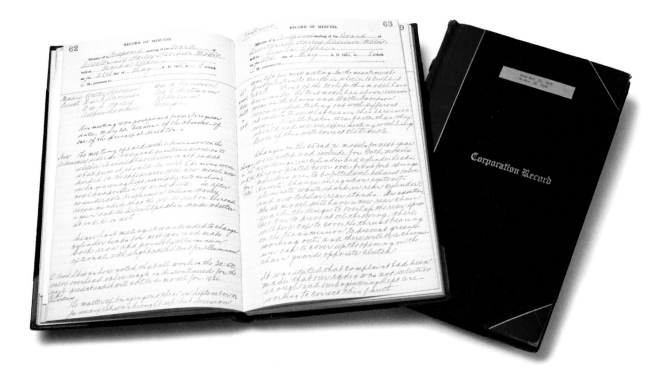

BOARD MEETING MINUTES FROM MAY 29, 1935. THE CRITICAL PASSAGE READS: "THE MATTER OF BRINGING OUT THE SIXTY-ONE IN SEPTEMBER OR JANUARY WAS BROUGHT UP BUT DECISION WAS LEFT FOR NEXT MEETING. IN THE MEANTIME THE FIRST QUESTION TO DECIDE IS WHETHER TO BUILD IT AT ALL."

combustion chambers, and a dry-sump oil system, that was radically advanced compared to Harley-Davidson's outdated, side-valve, total-loss Flathead designs.

Motor Company officials called it alternately the Sixty-One (refering to its displacement in cubic inches) or the Overhead (regarding its valvetrain); today, we know it as the Knucklehead (in reference to polished aluminum rocker boxes that look like the knuckles on a clenched fist). Whatever you call it, the EL is one of the most gorgeous and timeless motorcycles ever built, and one that still inspires Harley-Davidson designers today.

Dealers knew they were looking at something special. After a few seconds of stunned silence, the ballroom erupted in wave after wave of enthusiastic applause. They had been waiting half a decade for new product to sell. Harley-Davidson had finally delivered— and then some. Though the crowd was thrilled, behind the scenes, Harley and the rest of the Motor Company leadership were less than confident.

Development of this new model had proceeded in fits and starts, and the consensus inside Juneau Avenue was that the Sixty-One was not ready for primetime. Though officially under

THE FOUR FOUNDERS INSPECT ONE OF THE FIRST EL
KNUCKLEHEAD MODELS AS IT ROLLS OFF THE ASSEMBLY
LINE. FROM LEFT TO RIGHT: ARTHUR DAVIDSON,
WALTER DAVIDSON, WILLIAM A. DAVIDSON, AND
WILLIAM S. HARLEY.

development for four years, the project had been delayed and derailed repeatedly due to a lack of funding. Board meeting notes reveal that company executives considered scrapping the Overhead project entirely as late as May of 1935, only to rush it into production shortly after. The first official prototypes weren't assembled until September of 1935, and initial testing was not promising. The Sixty-One engines were very fast, for sure, but the overhead-valve top ends leaked oil—a lot of oil—and a fix was not obvious. Still, the company charged forward.

Harley-Davidson was understandably cautious with the rollout. Dealers were sworn to secrecy after that November conference, and when the 1936 model-year flyer appeared a few weeks later, it didn't even mention the Sixty-One. The 1936 model-year announcements in *The Enthusiast* magazine likewise made no mention of any new model. It was as if the bike never existed. The first production Sixty-Ones were assembled in January of 1936, but dealers weren't encouraged to place orders.

Then, on February 2, a little-known racer, Butch Quirk, won a 350-mile endurance race in Portland, Oregon, riding a sidecar-equipped EL. Real-world success like this—and a deafening buzz from dealers and consumers alike—slightly calmed corporate anxiety. Harley-Davidson began officially taking orders for the Sixty-One on February 21, though the first shipments were delayed until late March—when oil leakage was finally cured with new valve stem covers and vacuum-operated breather valves. By June, the Motor Company was taking orders faster than it could build bikes. Harley-Davidson's original hope was to sell 1,600 Overheads that first year; the company actually sold 1,700, despite all the problems and delays. Depression? What Depression? The Sixty-One was an immediate success.

And why not? The 1936 EL was an instant classic, debuting iconic styling cues that can still be seen on Harley-Davidson's most popular models today. A distinctive line stretches straight back from the steering head to the rear axle and perfectly defines that iconic hardtail line. Look at a modern Softail and you'll see an echo of that same perfect line. The 45-degree V-twin, with twin chromed pushrod tubes plunging straight downward from polished aluminum rocker boxes, looks essentially just like the latest Milwaukee Eight. Tank-mounted instruments were a new innovation on the EL model too, crowned here with a 100-mile-per-hour speedometer placed front and center where everyone could see it. And yes, the Sixty-One could easily bury that needle.

The success of the Sixty-One displayed Harley-Davidson's ability to innovate even in times of great adversity, a characteristic that would prove vital to the company's survival many times in the succeeding decades. Consumer demand for the Sixty-One drove total sales to 11,674 in 1937, a remarkable rebound, and sales of the overhead-valve Knucklehead would remain strong enough to carry the Motor Company through another economic challenge—World War II—less than a decade later. By the end of 1947, Harley-Davidson was once again selling more than twenty thousand motorcycles per year—more than half of which (eleven thousand) were Knuckleheads.

18

JOE PETRALI AND THE BLUE STREAK

Call Joe Petrali a one-man Wrecking Crew. Though he didn't join forces with Harley-Davidson until 1925—long after business and politics had forced the Motor Company to dismantle the original Wrecking Crew—Petrali was essentially unbeatable on any surface, from board tracks to dirt tracks to hillclimbs. He was one of the greatest motorcycle racers that ever lived, winning a remarkable forty-nine national championship races before he retired in 1938—a mark that wasn't bested until 1992, when Harley-Davidson flat-track racer Scott Parker won his fiftieth AMA national.

Petrali won the first race he ever entered, a nationally sanctioned economy run, at age fourteen. He got his first professional opportunity with Indian at the Pacific Coast Championship in 1921—replacing the legendary Shrimp Burns, who had tragically lost his life at a race in Toledo, Ohio, the week before. He won many races for Indian and Excelsior both before joining the Harley-Davidson squad. His introduction to Harley-Davidson was accidental, when his factory Indian racer was lost in transit on the way to a board-track race at Altoona, Pennsylvania (his bike was shipped to Pittsburgh by mistake). Petrali borrowed a Harley-Davidson race bike from Ralph Hepburn, who had broken his hand in a practice crash, and promptly won the 100-mile championship race and shattered a speed record in the process.

Harley-Davidson signed Petrali immediately, and a few weeks later he won three national titles (10-, 25-, and 50-mile titles in the 61-cubic-inch class) at Laurel, Maryland, on September 7, 1925. Petrali was essentially a one-man factory team for most of the next decade. From May through August of 1935, Petrali won every Class A national race—thirteen in a row. The combination of Petrali and Harley-Davidson was unbeatable.

So, it made perfect sense that when Chief Engineer William Harley wanted to drum up some publicity around the recently revealed Knucklehead engine, Petrali was the person he called. Together with Harley-Davidson Racing Engineer Hank Syvertson, Petrali created this highly modified land-speed racer dubbed the *Blue Streak*. Though based on a standard EL-model motorcycle and powered by the 61-cubic-inch overhead-valve engine, *Blue Streak* was highly modified with dual carburetors, high-compression pistons, different cams, and a hot magneto, and it was tuned to run on alcohol, which burns faster than gasoline. Drop handlebars frame a fairing fashioned from a cut-down teardrop fuel tank, and a disc wheel cover cleans up the airflow around the front wheel. An enclosed tail section conceals the back half of the bike—though the tail section had to be removed for the official record attempt, because it actually caused serious vehicle instability.

In early March of 1937, Petrali and his crew set off for the hard-packed sands of Daytona Beach, Florida, to make an attempt on the absolute speed record for two-wheeled vehicles. On the morning of March 13, Petrali suited up and blasted the *Blue Streak* to an ultimate top speed of 136.183 miles per hour, setting a new land-speed record and making "Smokin' Joe" Petrali the fastest man on two wheels. Petrali's record stood for eleven years—the same amount of time the Knucklehead remained in production—and wasn't bested until Rollie Free broke the mark on a Vincent Black Lightning at the Bonneville Salt Flats in 1948. No one has

ever gone faster than Smokin' Joe on the Daytona sand, though. Petrali was the last great Class A racer, having spent his entire career riding high-dollar, purpose-built factory racing machines. By 1938, Class A was dead, replaced by the Class C racing formula that favored lightly modified production motorcycles that were more accessible to less experienced riders. Petrali raced one and only one Class C event, the Oakland 200, in November 1938. After almost being hit too many times, he pulled off the track, hung up his leathers, and walked away from racing for good.

Petrali's retirement marked the end of a legendary era, but his adventures didn't stop when he quit racing motorcycles. He soon took a position working as a flight engineer with Hughes Aircraft Company, where he helped eccentric billionaire business tycoon Howard Hughes develop the legendary *Spruce Goose*, the largest "flying boat" ever built. Petrali also worked as a crew chief for several Indy 500 teams, acted as a land-speed racing official at the Bonneville Salt Flats, and famously traveled everywhere carrying a membership card that identified him as American Motorcyclist Association Life Member No. 1.

More HILLCLIMB VICTORIES *for* HARLEY-DAVIDSON

IN the point hillclimb competition which ended Aug. 30, Herb Reiber and Windy Lindstrom, the two famous Harley-Davidson pros, outclassed the entire field. Each won more points and more first places than any other pro. riders in the country. In fact, Harley-Davidson won more points than all other makes combined.

And in the amateur ranks, Oliver Clow, Oke Hedman and D. Jenkins each won high point honors in their sections. Clow and Hedman together accounted for 14 first places out of a possible 20 in the 45 Amateur events. Harley-Davidson riders headed the official A.M.A. point standings in 6 of the 7 sections.

Here are some of the high spots in the month's competition victories:

AUGUST 16, 1931
At Louisville, Ky., Ralph Moore accounted for two firsts for Harley-Davidson, winning both the 45 and 61 events. Moore was the only rider over the top. Harley-Davidson riders also took first and second in the 80 Amateur.

At Port Jervis, N. Y., on the same day, Herb Reiber assured himself of ten more points with firsts in both professional events. Hedman snatched five more with a win in the 45 Amateur.

At San Francisco, Harley-Davidson riders made a clean sweep, winning every event. Lindstrom took both the 45 and 61 events, Clow the 45 Amateur and Herb the 80 Amateur.

AUGUST 23, 1931
At Omaha, Nebr., it was 3 out of 3 for Harley-Davidson.

At Vallejo, Calif., Lindstrom set a new hill record in the 45 Pro. and Joe Herb copped the 80 Amateur.

At the Cincinnati, O., races, Harley-Davidson riders won every event.

AUGUST 30, 1931
At Bethlehem, Pa., Oke Hedman, star Harley-Davidson amateur rider, showed his stuff with firsts in both the amateur events.

At Princeton, Ill., McClintock and his Harley-Davidson took them all to the cleaners in both the 45 Pro. and 61 Expert events.

At San Diego, Calif., Windy Lindstrom and Joe Herb copped the 61 Pro. and 80 Amateur events.

HARLEY-DAVIDSON MOTOR CO.
MILWAUKEE   WISCONSIN

. . . . RIDE A HARLEY-DAVIDSON AND YOU RIDE A WINNER!

ABOVE—Joe Petrali and his Harley-Davidson going over the top of Mt. Garfield, the famous sand dune at Muskegon, Michigan. This picture was snapped just as Joe won the 61 Pro. event at the point hillclimb held there on August 23rd.
Two weeks before, on August 9th, at the Milwaukee State Fair Track, Petrali and his Harley-Davidson copped both the 5-mile and the 10-mile Pro. races. On hill or track this combination of skill and horsepower is mighty hard to beat.

HARLEY—DAVIDSON
Enthusiast

APRIL, 1937

HARLEY—DAVIDSON
SETS NEW RECORD OF
136.183
MILES PER HOUR

Joe Petrali Pilots 61 OHV Harley-Davidson to New Record of 136.183 M.P.H. at Daytona Beach.

★

102.047 M.P.H. Class C Straightaway Record Set With Harley-Davidson Stock 45 Twin Model.

★

Records Made Both Ways of Course, Electrically Timed, and Officially Certified by A.M.A.

★

Records Were Made With Non-Supercharged Motors.

DAYTONA BEACH, FLORIDA, MARCH 13 • This was a red-letter day for motorcycle speed when Joe Petrali set two new American Motorcycle Association straightaway records — 136.183 miles per hour with a 61 OHV of stock design and 102.047 miles per hour with a Class C 45 stock Twin. These remarkable times were made both ways of a one-mile surveyed course, electrically timed by John LaTour, the same man who timed Sir Malcolm Campbell, and were refereed by E. C. Smith, Secretary of the A.M.A.

The 136.183 m.p.h. record Petrali established with a four-valve 61 OHV decidedly exceeds the speed of 132.01 m.p.h. established by John Seymour riding an eight-valve 61 overhead of other make over a one-kilometer course, approximately 5⁄8 of a mile, made on Daytona Beach January 12, 1926. The 102.04 m.p.h. record made with a stock 45 Twin beats the former record of Jesse James, riding another make motorcycle, made March 1, 1935, at Daytona Beach over a one-mile course.

Neither of the Harley-Davidsons ridden by Petrali was fitted with a supercharger. Every rule and stipulation of the A.M.A. Competition Rules was strictly adhered to in establishing these records and they have been officially certified. They were made on merit and performance and again demonstrate most emphatically the speed, stamina, dependability, and outstanding superiority of the Harley-Davidson motorcycles.

HARLEY-DAVIDSON MOTOR COMPANY • MILWAUKEE, WISCONSIN, U. S. A.

19

HOW CAN HARLEY-DAVIDSON SERVE YOU?

From the earliest days of motorized transportation, motorcycles were a natural solution for commercial work—faster than a horse and buggy and more economical than an early car or truck. Consider this endorsement from mail carrier David Louder, which was used in a 1915 Harley-Davidson advertisement: "Before buying a Harley-Davidson, I kept four ponies and a mail wagon. Now I keep one horse and my Harley-Davidson, who doesn't seem to have any appetite for corn or alfalfa, and yet makes the same trip on the route in one-third of the time with an expense of about ten cents a day."

Working motorcycles have been a part of the Harley-Davidson lineup since 1913, when the Motor Company released its first Motorcycle Truck, the Model G Forecar. Essentially a reverse trike built from a 61-cubic-inch motorcycle with two front wheels separated by a large service box, Harley-Davidson built just 332 Forecars between 1913 and 1915, before these were discontinued and replaced with the more versatile Package Truck utility sidecar. Hugely popular with small businesses offering delivery service, the Package Truck came from the factory with a standard cargo box, but many customers outfitted the chassis with their own customized cargo carriers shaped to accommodate any sort of load. By 1916—when a new law permitting rural postal carriers who rode motorcycles to use a Package Truck—the US Postal Service fleet grew to more than 4,700 Harley-Davidson Package Trucks. One of these is installed permanently in the Harley-Davidson Museum.

HARLEY-DAVIDSON
SERVI-CAR
» » » » »

» » » » » THE MODERN METHOD FOR PROFITABLE PICK-UP AND DELIVERY OF AUTOMOBILES ....

SAVES AN EXTRA MAN'S TIME ....

Servi-Car does away with the need for sending out two men and a car to pick up or deliver a customer's automobile. It saves the cost of one man's wages and doubles and trebles the profits on the other man's working time.

» » SAVES HIGH CAR EXPENSE ...

Cuts down the gas, oil, tire and depreciation cost of pick-up and delivery with a car. Prevents the losses occasioned through use of service or tow cars in this work, when that equipment can be used more profitably elsewhere.

» » ANYONE CAN OPERATE IT ....

Servi-Car can be driven by anyone in your present organization. Avoids the necessity of hiring inefficient transient drivers during rush periods. Permits sending out employees especially adept in handling certain customer contracts.

» » » INCREASES SERVICE SALES ...

Convenient pick-up and delivery enables your service manager to sell many service jobs that might not come to you otherwise. Specials featured by telephone or advertising will be taken advantage of by many more customers.

» » » EFFECTIVE ADVERTISING ...

Servi-Car's eye-catching appearance, plus the message that can be easily lettered on it, is one of the most effective advertising mediums you could employ. Every pick-up and delivery is an advertisement reaching a multitude of prospects.

During the Great Depression, working motorcycles became more important for Harley-Davidson than ever before. As so-called pleasure sales plummeted, commercial vehicle sales became essential to the Motor Company's survival. Customers would invest in vehicles that could help them make money, so Harley-Davidson responded with an all-new utility model, dubbed the Servi-Car, in 1932. Businesses looking for economical and efficient delivery options flocked to the Servi-Car, and it went on to become one of the most long-lived vehicles in the Motor Company's history. Unlike previous Motorcycle Truck or Package Car designs, the Servi-Car was a conventional trike with one wheel in the front and two in the rear. This design made it much easier to handle, especially at higher speeds—greatly expanding its appeal.

The Servi-Car was conceived as the "ideal commercial vehicle" and initially marketed as a means for automobile dealerships to attract customers and reduce costs. Period advertisements highlighted the Servi-Car's economy, generous cargo capacity, and the fact that anyone could drive one. The hand-lettered 1939 Model G Servi-Car on display at the Harley-Davidson Museum exhibit formerly belonged to John Stanton, who purchased it in 1938 to make house calls for his Babylon, New York, Dodge-Plymouth car dealership. Stanton or one of his mechanics would ride the Servi-Car to a customer's home to retrieve a vehicle in need of service, using a special tow bar mounted to the front axle that attached to the car's rear bumper in order to tow the Servi-Car back to the shop. Pickup and delivery of cars was now a one-man job, improving efficiency and profitability. Later versions could be equipped with additional accessories intended specifically for auto repair shops, including an air tank and pressure gauge for on-the-spot tire repairs, as well as a combo rear bumper/spare tire carrier.

The Servi-Car proved especially popular with law enforcement too, aided by the fact that Harley-Davidson had so many strong and successful relationships with police departments across the nation. Affordable, reliable, and small enough to navigate

small spaces and not obstruct traffic while the officer checked parked cars, the Servi-Car soon became a mainstay for the law enforcement community. A full line of optional accessories designed specifically for police use—including a heel-activated siren that ran off the rear wheel, shielded spark-plug cables to prevent radio interference, and red and blue "pursuit" lighting—further increased functionality for law enforcement agencies.

The remarkable longevity of the Servi-Car platform (and the 45-cubic-inch flathead engine that powered it) is the ultimate endorsement of Harley-Davidson's utility-bike concept. Servi-Car production began in 1932 and ended forty-one years later, in 1973—a Harley-Davidson longevity record now topped only by the Sportster and Electra Glide models. It was an inspired—and hugely successful—strategy to expand Harley-Davidson's core business beyond consumer transportation, pulling the Motor Company through many very hard times. It's widely agreed that Harley-Davidson likely would not have survived the Depression without the Servi-Car sales to boost the bottom line, and steady commercial sales helped carry the Motor Company through more difficult times in the decades that followed.

20

UNCLE SAM'S IRON PONY

Before the Great Depression, upwards of forty established motorcycle manufacturers were in the United States, including such great names as the Flying Merkel, Thor, Iver-Johnson, Pierce, Pope, Yale, and many, many more. After the Great Depression, only three were left, and when the combined Excelsior and Henderson operations ceased production on March 31, 1931, only two American motorcycle manufacturers remained: Indian and Harley-Davidson. Both just barely survived the Great Depression, subsisting mostly on commercial business, and by the late 1930s, both had made solid—if not spectacular—recoveries, with production returning to roughly pre-Depression levels.

Then America's next great economic challenge—World War II—reared its ugly, fascist head. One of these two manufacturers—the one that won a lucrative government contract—would thrive; the other would enter into a deep and ultimately irreversible decline.

The Harley-Davidson Motor Company was no stranger to military service. The Motor Company's first engagement with the US Army was in 1916, when it supplied a few hundred J models to assist General John "Black Jack" Pershing and his Eighth Brigade during the Mexican Border Campaign, pursuing Mexican revolutionary Pancho Villa around the deserts of Northern Mexico after Villa launched an attack on the US city of Columbus, New Mexico. Pershing never caught Villa, but the performance of the Harley-Davidson motorcycles was so impressive that the

US Army eventually ordered eight thousand bikes—a third of the company's production during that period—to support overseas efforts during World War I, making Harley-Davidson "Uncle Sam's Choice."

It wasn't surprising then that when the United States began ramping up its support of World War II in the early 1940s, the US government offered Harley-Davidson a contract to create a special, battle-ready motorcycle for the US and other Allied forces. Harley-Davidson responded with a heavy-duty version of its civilian WL model, powered by the stone reliable, 45-cubic-inch Flathead V-twin. Called the WLA, this rugged warhorse was upgraded for battle with a heavier frame, a lower headlight, and thicker handlebar tubes than the civilian WL. Other changes included an oil-bath air filter for better dust protection, skirtless fenders to prevent mud buildup, and an optional separate lighting system equipped with metal black-out visors to camouflage the bike after dark. Though often seen with a gun scabbard attached to the front fork, the WLA was never intended as a combat

vehicle. These were used almost exclusively for dispatch and courier duties, so the machine gun was strictly for protection.

Nicknamed "Uncle Sam's Iron Pony," the soon-to-be-ubiquitous WLA played some role in nearly every World War II campaign. With so many resources being dedicated to other wartime industries, many US allies could no longer afford to build their own bikes. Harley-Davidson willingly filled the gap, supplying motorcycles not only to every branch of the US military, but also the armed forces of New Zealand, France, Canada, South Africa, China, Australia, Brazil, Russia, and more. In fact, more than one third of all WLAs manufactured by Harley-Davidson were delivered to Russia through the United States' Lend-Lease policy. Harley-Davidson motorcycles played an essential role during the World War II, with mounted riders performing communications, reconnaissance, transportation, and combat duties—including many crucial tasks for the legendary "Hell on Wheels" Second Armored Division, commanded by Col. George S. Patton Jr.

Standard-issue WLA repair kit

Return to Desk E-6

THE ARMORED SCHOOL

Motorcycle Department

Fort Knox, Ky.

MOTORCYCLE MECHANICS
HANDBOOK   1943

TM 9-1879

WAR DEPARTMENT TECHNICAL MANUAL

ORDNANCE MAINTENANCE

MOTORCYCLE, SOLO

(HARLEY-DAVIDSON MODEL WLA)

RESTRICTED

Dissemination of restricted matter.—The information contained in
restricted documents and the essential characteristics of restricted
materiel may be given to any person known to be in the service
of the United States and to persons of undoubted loyalty and discre-
tion who are cooperating in Government work, but will not be
communicated to the public or to the press except by authorized
military public relations agencies. (See also paragraph 18b, AR
380-5, 28 September 1942.)

WAR DEPARTMENT

29 MARCH 1944

Harley-Davidson even converted its Service School into a training facility for military personnel during wartime—the Quartermaster School was open again—teaching all aspects of repair, including how to service motorcycles under harsh field conditions and with limited tools. In total, more than one hundred thousand soldiers were trained to operate and repair Harley-Davidson motorcycles during World War II.

At the same time, as the US Armed Forces and their allies were buying as many WLAs as they could get their hands on, the US government also gave the Motor Company special orders in March of 1941 to design an all-new motorcycle purpose-built to withstand the harshest desert conditions. The resulting XA model (XS when equipped with a sidecar) is one of the more unique Harley-Davidsons ever built and one of very few Harley-Davidson motorcycles that doesn't use a V-twin engine. Instead, it's powered by a horizontally opposed flat-twin engine similar

to the desert-ready BMW motorcycles used by German forces in the North African campaign.

The opposed-twin engine was selected because it offered certain design advantages in extreme conditions, namely that both cylinders stuck out beyond the outer frame rails, where they were bathed in fresh, cooling air. Also similar to the BMW, the XA utilized a sealed-shaft drive that was impervious to desert sand; a second sealed-shaft assembly drove the sidecar wheel for extra traction and power.

The US government originally contracted Harley-Davidson to build one thousand shaft-driven motorcycles, demanding a delivery date not later than July of 1942. Harley-Davidson only built three XS prototypes before the government cancelled this order, however, deciding to order 44 Jeeps for desert warfare instead. Military leadership then deemed the standard WLA "satisfactory for all future military motorcycle requirements." The XS displayed in the museum collection today is thought to be the only surviving example.

Effects of the war were not limited to overseas conflict—Harley-Davidson faced numerous wartime challenges at home too. The nationwide labor shortage was one issue. Many Motor Company employees were drafted into service, of course, requiring the firm to hire women for the first time to fill vacancies on the factory floor—a cultural shift. Women handled many vital tasks—operating machinery, assembling bikes, and inspecting and packaging parts.

Material rationing also affected what Harley-Davidson was able to produce, and how they delivered it to market. Harley-Davidson oil had to be temporarily packaged in glass, for example, due to a wartime ban on the use of metals. Further material restrictions directly affected motorcycle production. Chrome parts were temporarily painted black, due to wartime metal restrictions, while rubber restrictions meant floorboard pads were eliminated and handgrips were made from plastic instead.

In total, Harley-Davidson built eighty thousand motorcycles—and $28 million worth of spare motorcycle parts—to support the war effort during the period between 1940 and V-J Day in 1945. The Motor Company produced very few civilian bikes during that same period. A press release from 1942 addressed this situation: "The Harley-Davidson you had hoped to ride . . . is out at the front helping to win the war. We know you are glad to forego your new dream motorcycle so the brave lads in Uncle Sam's forces are equipped with the latest and best." Civilian models changed very little from 1941 thorough 1946, while all the nation's materials and labor were consumed by the war effort. Engines, color choices, and even gas tank emblems on civilian bikes remained the same from year to year.

Meanwhile, Harley-Davidson's local production facilities were converted not only to produce war-ready bikes but also shell parts, truck components, and even some small parts for B-29 bombers.

This massive wartime contract was the key to Harley-Davidson's future success, pulling the Motor Company for once and for all out of the Depression-era doldrums and at the same time dooming its primary competitor, Indian, to financial ruin. American military success added a money-can't-buy luster to the Harley-Davidson brand, and positioned the Motor Company for huge success during the coming postwar boom. Though many dealers struggled to stay afloat during the war, those that survived were rewarded with crowds of returning servicemen—many who learned to ride in the service, on a Harley-Davidson—lining up to purchase brand-new bikes on which to enjoy their hard-earned freedom. At the same time, loads of cheap and available military surplus bikes—combined with a small population of bored, adrenaline-seeking ex-GIs—created a parallel outlaw motorcycle subculture.

Front Line Hero!

Make way in your hearts for another hero—Uncle Sam's motorcycle soldier. Astride his throbbing mount, he symbolizes the modern mechanized forces fighting for freedom .... Not only is he out far ahead scouting for priceless information about enemy positions, enemy strength, bridges, roads, tank traps, but he is also engaging in actual combat. Through enemy lines he breaks and leaves confusion, fear and terror in his wake. The skillful, daring riding so many of our army motorcyclists learned in competition on hill, road and track in days of peace is serving them well in these strenuous days of war. Their service to freedom's cause is beyond price. We salute our brave motorcycle soldiers .. are proud of them and their deeds. HARLEY-DAVIDSON MOTOR COMPANY, Milwaukee, Wis., U.S.A.

BACK HIM UP WITH BONDS!

... Somewhere in France

The Enthusiast

A MAGAZINE FOR MOTORCYCLISTS

SEPTEMBER 1944

21

BIRTH OF THE BIKER

By the end of the war, military surplus bikes (and parts) were scattered all over the globe. Many came back to the States, where they were adapted for civilian use. Others stayed where they were, adding even more international riders to the Harley-Davidson family. No matter what the geographic location, many of these surplus bikes were modified, in effect creating the modern custom motorcycle movement.

From the beginning, there were two tribes of motorcycle customizers: one group who preferred to add accessories to decorate and personalize their rides, and another that took parts off of their motorcycles in pursuit of more speed and increased thrills. For the former group, Harley-Davidson rushed to create a complete line of custom accessories, including chromed disc wheel covers, heavily fringed saddlebags, seat covers, and more. There is an unrestored 1947 FL model in the museum collection that is decorated in this style. The latter group did the exact opposite and focused their attention on removing parts to reduce weight and increase acceleration. Removing the front fender and all safety equipment and then cutting short the rear fender created a bobber—the predecessor to the choppers that became wildly popular in the 1960s and '70s.

Nowhere was the bobber style more popular or prevalent than in Southern California, which in the years following the end of World War II was gripped by a hot-rodding boom of epic proportions. The bike of choice for this crowd was a cheap-and-available military surplus WLA, bobbed for speed. This hot-rod/bobber culture extended beyond vehicles. It represented a lifestyle, one that existed on the fringes of polite society and one that was especially attractive to a certain disaffected portion of the returning military population that wasn't quite ready to settle into buttoned-down suburban life.

Many of these hot-rod hoodlums soon gathered together and formed the original "outlaw" (non-AMA-sanctioned) motorcycle clubs, or MCs. One of the very first outlaw MCs, which formed in late-'40s in Los Angeles, called themselves "The Boozefighters." That name says it all. Many of the original Boozefighters—including "Wino" Willie Forkner, who founded the Motorcycle Club with his friend John Cameron, who was rejected by the military because his body was compromised from too many motorcycle crashes—were returning World War II vets who were bored and desperate for thrills. They found what they were seeking by buying ex-military WLAs for next to nothing, stripping off all the military gear, and building fast and indestructible bobbers to ride and race on the dry lakes of Southern California. A 1942 WLA bobber replica, built in the style of an original Boozefighters bike complete with the signature green-and-white color scheme and the club's three-star bottle logo on the oil tank, is part of the museum collection today.

Over the Fourth of July weekend in 1947, the Boozefighters and a bunch of similar outlaw MCs, including the Pissed Off Bastards, the Market Street Commandos, the Top Hatters, and the Galloping Goose Motorcycle Club, decided to crash the party at a Gypsy Tour rally in Hollister, California. More than four thousand motorcyclists arrived in town that weekend—almost doubling the local population. Most came to watch the races and participate in polite social activities, but a small minority like the Boozefighters, came exclusively to party and make noise, drinking, fighting, and racing their unmuffled motorcycles up and down narrow city streets. The result was pure chaos, captured for the entire nation to see in a sensational article published in the July 21 issue of *Life* magazine, which simultaneously condemned and created the legend of the outlaw biker. This outlaw archetype was further celebrated in the iconic Marlon Brando film *The Wild One*—said to be inspired by the 1947 Hollister riot—and the outlaw survives and even still thrives today, some seventy years later.

Backlash to the infamous Hollister incident was almost immediate, as evidenced by this quote from a speech at the Harley-Davidson Dealer's Conference in November, 1947: "Well-dressed motorcycle riders on shiny, good-looking motorcycles are likely to stay out of trouble. Riders dressed in overalls, on motorcycles that are stripped down and generally dilapidated, are all dressed up for trouble and likely to find it." Before World War II, motorcycle clubs were generally a well-behaved bunch that took great pride in their organization and appearance. After the war, things were very different.

After experiencing the hell of combat, many returning servicemen just weren't ready to reenter normal life. Outlaw motorcycle clubs offered an alternative lifestyle characterized by speed, thrills, and regular opportunities to challenge the straight world of law-abiding citizens. The outlaw biker almost instantly became a major figure in American counterculture, and he maintained that position for many decades, with an influence, attitude, and aesthetic that still remains powerful and compelling even today.

22

DRESSED TO IMPRESS

We recognize motorcycling now as an equal-opportunity activity. Anyone, young or old, male or female, black or white, is encouraged to take up two-wheeled travel. This wasn't always the case, however. Like so many aspects of American life in the 1930s, motorcycling was segregated by race (and often by gender too). An American Motorcyclist Association membership application from 1930 on display at the museum drives this ugly reality home with bold print that clearly states: "membership limited to white persons only." Racial segregation wasn't limited to just lunch counters and drinking fountains—it affected the world of motorcycling too.

Of course, racist restrictions didn't stop African American enthusiasts from exercising their passion for motorcycling. It just led black riders to develop their own parallel universe of African American motorcycle clubs, many of which survive and thrive still today. One of the earliest of these was the Berkeley Tigers, an African American MC formed in California's Bay Area in the 1940s. The Berkeley Tigers, like many motorcycle clubs at that time, started as a drill team. Club members practiced synchronized riding in tight formations and performed trick riding in parades and competitions.

Each of these teams wore matching uniforms, and the look— or "colors"—of the uniform soon came to define the club. The Harley-Davidson Museum collection includes dozens of club sweaters contained in a large glass case in the Clubs and Competition gallery, and one of the most striking is the green-and-gold Berkeley Tigers sweater donated by club member Leo Hopkins. Hopkins, who began riding with the club in the mid-1940s, donated his Berkeley Tigers sweater along with an amazing collection of period photos and film footage depicting club activities and adventures. The Hopkins collection is a fascinating glimpse into the close-knit African American motorcycle culture as it existed in the late 1940s through the 1950s, a time when many motorcycle dealerships still refused to sell a motorcycle to a black person and an entire population was forced to create its own culture from scratch.

Other club sweaters featured in the Museum Collection present a comprehensive overview of the countless AMA-sanctioned motorcycle clubs that thrived in the period post–World War II—clubs such as Worcester, Massachusetts' Friendly Riders, which presented the exact opposite image of the Boozefighters and other troublemaking outlaw gangs that sprung up during the same period. AMA-sanctioned clubs appealed to better-adjusted Americans who enjoyed the camaraderie and compatibility that group participation in motorcycling could provide. Life in the AMA-sanctioned clubs was ruled by strict bylaws and revolved around regular club meetings that incorporated riding, whether in the form of poker runs, bike rodeos, or participation in larger regional "Gypsy tours."

Each of these clubs had a name, a charter, and, most importantly, its own formal, head-to-toe uniform. The museum exhibit includes club wear from around the country, including: the

Teadrinkers from Denver, Colorado; the Gopher State Motorcycle Club from Brooklyn Center, Minnesota; a blue sweater with a depiction of a duck holding an umbrella from the Tacoma MC in Tacoma, Washington; and the Beer City Riders from the Motor Company's hometown of Milwaukee (where else?). There are also club sweaters (and numerous photos) from the Motor Maids, one of the oldest and largest all-female motorcycle clubs, cofounded in 1940 by Linda Dugeau and Harley-Davidson dealer Dot Robinson.

Harley-Davidson Motor Company supported the sanctioned club scene almost from the very beginning, understanding that promoting sociability among motorcyclists is one of the easiest and most effective ways to promote the sport of motorcycling. One of the earliest artifacts in the club area is a pamphlet titled "Motorcycle Club: Constitution and By-Laws," published by Harley-Davidson in 1922. In the late 1930s, Harley-Davidson even offered a separate accessories flyer featuring suggested club uniform fabric swatches. Some of the customized sweaters on display in the museum were made by Harley-Davidson, which by this time offered complete special-ordered uniforms, including shirts, pants, and even "riding caps"—obviously, helmets were not yet considered required equipment at that time.

1948
NATIONAL
HARLEY-DAVIDSON
DEALERS' CONFERENCE

NOVEMBER 24–26 ● 1947

SCHROEDER HOTEL
MILWAUKEE · WISCONSIN

1948

HARLEY-DAVIDSON MOTOR CO.

JOSEPH G. KILBERT
DOMESTIC SALES MANAGER

NATIONAL DEALERS CONFERENCE

23

HARLEY-DAVIDSON'S WORLD OF TOMORROW

Big changes were coming to the Harley-Davidson Motor Company for the 1948 model year, and dealers were given their first peek behind the curtain during what was billed as a "top secret" 1947 Dealer Convention at Milwaukee. William H. Davidson, president of Harley-Davidson from 1942 through 1971, officially dubbed this stunt "Operation Secret Destination." On the evening of November 24, 1947, dealers and their guests were shuttled to the Chicago & North Western Railway depot in downtown Milwaukee. There, they boarded train coaches for an 8-mile ride to the nearby city of Wauwatosa, where they toured the new Capitol Drive manufacturing plant, recently constructed for the not-insignificant cost of $1.5 million.

"We have pledged ourselves to a far-reaching expansion program to maintain Harley-Davidson leadership," Davidson announced to the assembled dealers. "Now you see with your own eyes what we mean—not a blueprint, but this modern plant."

The cutting-edge manufacturing facility wasn't the only big news that Harley-Davidson executives had to share with the assembled dealers that evening. Company officials also revealed for the first time an all-new motorcycle—the diminutive, 125cc S model that would at last provide Harley-Davidson a low-cost, entry-level motorcycle and an economical offering to satisfy the booming postwar global transportation market. A radical departure from the existing big twin line, the S model was a key part of a new vision for the future of the Harley-Davidson Motor Company—something William H. Davidson referred to as the "Harley-Davidson World of Tomorrow"—that included of new and more relevant products, enhanced services, and a more modern factory to satisfy the pent-up global demand for Harley-Davidson motorcycles.

World War II produced many positive side effects for Harley-Davidson. Military production kept the business in the black throughout the war years, and further positioned the brand for success when tens of thousands of ex-GIs returned to civilian life and wanted motorcycles to enjoy their newfound leisure time. Harley-Davidson produced almost no civilian machines during the war—nearly all production went toward the war effort—but production shifted into overdrive after the war was over, increasing on average by four thousand bikes per year from 1945 to 1948. The postwar era saw an economic boom in America, and Harley-Davidson was better positioned than most to take advantage. For the first time in many years, motorcycling was once again a part of mainstream culture and the Motor Company responded enthusiastically with new products and renewed efforts to expand into the emerging new youth market.

At the same time, the spoils of war—in the form of war reparations—allowed a significant product expansion for the Motor Company, instantly creating a lightweight product line to supply the demand for cheap and efficient transportation both in America and abroad. This new S model was based on the DKW RT125, the drawings for which were seized from Nazi Germany as war reparations after the conclusion of World War II. (The RT125 drawings were also given to the United Kingdom and the Soviet Union, resulting in the BSA Bantam and MMZ Moskya/Minsk, respectively.) Powered by a 125cc two-stroke single that produced just 3 horsepower and riding on girder forks suspended by large rubber bands, the simple and relatively inexpensive (just $325) S model rapidly gained a huge following among young riders—so much that a remarkable ten thousand S models were sold in the first year alone. "Never before has a brand-new Harley-Davidson enjoyed such success in its first year," President William H. Davidson happily exclaimed at his annual address to stockholders in 1948.

The S model and other lightweight products continued to be successful for Harley-Davidson, opening the dealership doors to women, younger riders, commuters, and anyone else put off by the size or expense of a big twin motorcycle. In fact, by 1955, lightweights accounted for fully a third of Harley-Davidson's annual production. But competing in this rapidly changing market wasn't without

1948

its challenges, as European brands became more and more popular with American motorcycle buyers. In the early 1950s, Harley-Davidson faced especially stiff competition from affordable lightweight bikes made by British manufacturers, including BSA, Triumph, and Norton. Harley-Davidson sold nearly thirty thousand motorcycles in 1948, but production dropped to a mere fifteen thousand by 1951—a 50-percent decrease that could be largely traced to the flood of cheaper European lightweight bikes pouring into the American market.

The United Kingdom experienced remarkable industrial growth after World War II, including expanded motorcycle production. British imports to the United States increased nearly thirty times over what they were before the war, and by 1951, bikes such as BSA's

Bantam 125 were routinely outselling Harley-Davidson's S models. The S model and the Bantam were essentially identical (remember, both were based on the same DKW RT125), but thanks to lower wages and a devalued currency in Britain, the BSA cost far less.

With higher manufacturing and labor expenses, Harley-Davidson struggled to compete. The Motor Company eventually turned to the US government for assistance, requesting tariff protection in the form of a higher customs duty on lightweight British motorcycles. Taxing the Brits, it was thought, would level the playing field and increase Harley-Davidson's domestic sales. The US government ultimately chose not to institute a tariff in 1951, however, leaving the Motor Company to fend for itself. (The US government did choose to institute a similar tariff in the

1980s, when Harley-Davidson faced increased competition from Japanese manufacturers.)

As a result, Harley-Davidson was forced to take active steps to better prepare its dealer network for the increasing sales challenges. "The days of just sitting around and taking orders are definitely gone," company leadership warned dealers in 1951. "We've got to go after sales by creating a demand for our products." The Motor Company responded with an aggressive "Get in on the good times now!" ad campaign, featuring young enthusiasts having the time of their lives on the company's lightweight motorcycle line.

To help make motorcycling even more accessible, Harley-Davidson created "Pay-As-You-Ride" financing options through their subsidiary Kilbourn Finance Corporation to assist young riders with smaller budgets to make a purchase—including a Club Plan that required no down payment. It was never easier to become a Harley-Davidson owner.

Harley-Davidson continued to manufacture RT125-based lightweight motorcycles until 1966, when the Bobcat—the last of these DKW-derived machines—was discontinued. A few years earlier, in 1960, Harley-Davidson had purchased a 50-percent share of Italian manufacturer Aermacchi's motorcycle division. Harley-Davidson eventually replaced its entire lineup of outdated, American-made two-strokes with more modern Aermacchi machines, including a 250cc, four-stroke single that was rebadged as the Harley-Davidson Sprint. The highly capable and popular Sprint was upsized to 350cc in 1969 and remained in production until 1974—the same year that Harley-Davidson purchased full control of Aermacchi's motorcycle division, which they eventually sold to Cagiva in 1978.

24

THE HYDRA-GLIDE

This motorcycle—the 1949 Harley-Davidson FL Hydra-Glide—is the bike that inspired a million imitations, both within Harley-Davidson's own styling department and, decades later, halfway around the world when Japanese manufacturers began building American-style heavyweight cruisers. It's the archetypal American motorcycle, with a timeless look that's just as compelling now as it was back then.

Harley-Davidson debuted its FL chassis—a variation of which, the Street Glide, is still its best-selling motorcycle today—way back in 1941. The Motor Company introduced the legendary Panhead engine, named for its rocker covers that look like upside-down baking pans, in 1948. But it wasn't until the following year, when the antique springer fork was replaced with a modern telescopic unit, that the quintessential American cruiser silhouette took form. Dubbed the "Hydra-Glide" in reference to the new hydraulic fork that delivered twice the travel of the old springer, this latest Big Twin offered much-improved ride quality and road-holding

ability. The new fork also imparted a modern look more in line with the telescopic-forked British bikes that were beginning to flood the American market.

The deep-skirted front fender and thick, widely spaced fork legs—the upper halves enclosed in a streamlined, stamped-steel nacelle—give the Hydra-Glide a broad-shouldered look that has never gone out of style. Not surprisingly, this front fork assembly was designed on contract by Brooks Stevens, an industrial design icon (and lifelong Milwaukee resident) who also designed countless automobiles, home appliances, and even the famous Oscar Mayer Wienermobile. The rest of the bike, including the Fat Bob–type tank with its center-located speedometer and the sprung saddle cantilevered high above a rigid rear triangle, is just as memorable. Compare a vintage Hydra-Glide to a modern Softail Deluxe and you'll count more similarities than differences. This is style with true staying power.

The Panhead engine represented a major upgrade from its Knucklehead predecessor, featuring lower-maintenance hydraulic valve lifters—the very first motorcycle to feature this technology—and aluminum cylinder heads, which were much easier to cool. Scarce and comparatively expensive before the war, aluminum became cheap and readily available after the war when thousands of surplus planes were flown home and melted down for raw materials. Switching from cast-iron to aluminum—a material with three times as much heat conductivity—greatly improved engine reliability. And while the new single-piece valve covers didn't completely cure the top-end oil leaks that plagued the Knucklehead—even after an internal felt "blanket" was added to create an additional oil barrier—the Panhead was still a more reliable, lower-maintenance engine than the old Knuckle, far and away.

The Hydra-Glide received incremental changes over the following years to further improve performance and reliability. The first major shift—no pun intended—arrived in 1951, when a foot shifter was finally offered as an option. Postwar British bikes made a foot shifter seem all but mandatory on a modern motorcycle, and even Indian, Harley-Davidson's last-remaining American competitor, had offered a foot-shift option on its Chief model since 1949. Harley-Davidson was careful to maintain a hand-shift option so as not to alienate hardcore traditionalists, but by 1954 foot-shifted bikes were outselling hand-shifted bikes by two-to-one. That

margin continued to grow, until Harley-Davidson finally phased out hand shifters completely in the late 1960s.

The Panhead engine received a major upgrade in 1955, when engineers boosted the compression ratio and added ported and polished intakes to create the FLH (H for high-compression), which offered a 10-percent increase in horsepower. The FLH was given even more power in 1956 with the addition of a hotter "Victory" camshaft and new pistons that provided yet another compression boost. FLH decals on either side of the oil tank announced to all who could see that this was officially Harley-Davidson's hot rod. This would ultimately be the final edition of the Hydra-Glide. The enormously popular model would be replaced by something even better in 1958—the Duo-Glide.

Before 1958, rear suspension on a Harley-Davidson Big Twin was limited to a sprung seat post that only suspended the rider. This was unacceptable by the late 1950s, by which time every imported motorcycle and even Harley-Davidson's smaller-displacement K and KH models came equipped with rear shocks. How could Harley-Davidson call its FLH the King of the Highway when the chassis could barely tame a speed bump? That all changed in 1958, when Harley-Davidson replaced the hardtail rear frame with a swingarm and twin hydraulically damped shock absorbers to create the Duo-Glide. The rear suspension finally matched the front, ride quality was vastly improved, and Harley-Davidson's Big Twin could now truthfully claim the title King of the Highway.

There was one final upgrade to Harley-Davidson's Big Twin platform that fully completed the transition from prewar antique to modern motorcycle, and that was the addition of electric start in 1965. After nearly two decades of competing with British bikes for technical superiority, Harley-Davidson now found itself competing

against another flood of imports, this time from Japan. Now the differentiating factor wasn't foot shifters or telescopic forks, but push-button starting—a game-changing innovation that Honda had quickly made the norm.

Kick-starting a large-displacement V-twin was a difficult and potentially deal-breaking ordeal for many would-be motorcyclists. Push-button starting removed a major barrier to entry, and this is one of many reasons why sales of Japanese bikes soared while Harley-Davidson motorcycles, once again, seemed out of date. Adding electric start to change the Duo-Glide into

the Electra-Glide fought this perception. Even though push-button technology added a hefty 75 pounds (!), buyers didn't seem to mind—first-year sales increased by 26 percent, making the Electra Glide the biggest selling Big Twin since 1951.

The Electra Glide was a better bike in every way. Smoother riding, more powerful, more reliable, and easy for anyone to start, the Electra-Glide appealed to an even broader cross-section of American riders, further extending Harley-Davidson's popularity among more casual riders and setting the stage for future brand longevity.

THE Enthusiast

MAY 1956

A MAGAZINE FOR MOTORCYCLISTS

ELVIS PRESLEY — Hottest singing style on wax. See story on page 14.

Who Is Elvis Presley?

THAT rocket blazing a fiery trail across the musical sky these days and nights is no rocket. It's 21 year old Elvis Presley, Memphis's contribution to the world of music. Presley's rise to fame has been little short of fantastic. Some time ago, Elvis walked into the Sun Record Company in Memphis, Tenn., and recorded his voice at his own expense. Sun Record Company liked Presley's style and signed him to a contract. Recently RCA Victor bought Presley's contract and he was on his way up. He recorded "Heartbreak Hotel". His unique style clicked at once. Now this record is a cinch to pass the million mark any day. He is in great demand for personal appearances and TV shows. More of his songs are being released. His head is in a whirl but Elvis is taking it all in stride. He appreciates his good fortune and is determined not to let it change him.

How does Elvis rate cover position in the ENTHUSIAST? He is a Harley-Davidson rider and is shown on his third motorcycle. He started out as the owner of a 165 and at present rides the 1956 "KH". It is a red and white model and is his favorite. His new life makes great demands on him but, he still finds time to roll up some miles on his "KH". Good luck for your future, Elvis. *Bruehl Photo*

Motorcycling on TV in San Diego, California

MOTORCYCLING received some good publicity in the San Diego area on March 30. Brad Andres, the 1955 Daytona Champion was interviewed and movies of motorcycling events were

THE KING'S K-MODEL

Nowadays it's almost a cliché, the breakout rock star celebrating his—or her—newfound success with a shiny new Harley-Davidson motorcycle. But back in 1956, when rock-and-roll was still in its infancy, Elvis Presley was the archetype. Just twenty-one years old, Presley was still a relatively unknown regional artist when he purchased this Pepper Red Harley-Davidson KH from Tommy Taylor at Memphis Harley-Davidson on January 14, 1956. This purchase marked a career milestone for Presley—the move from Sam Phillips's Sun Records to the major label RCA Victor.

Just four days earlier, Elvis had recorded his first song for RCA Victor, "Heartbreak Hotel," which went on to become a best-selling single and the basis for the first million-selling, number-one pop record—the eponymous *Elvis Presley*. Certainly, he had reason to celebrate.

The KH was not Elvis's first motorcycle, as many believe. His first motorcycle was a Harley Model 165 that he purchased in 1955 with the proceeds from his first Sun Records contract. In early 1956, with both his riding skills and his bank balance improving, he upgraded to the more powerful KH. Presley selected the two-tone Deluxe KH with the optional windshield and buddy seat, so he could give pretty girls rides. He paid $903 (after trading his Model 165) and financed that amount with a monthly payment of $47.

This is the bike Presley posed with on the cover of the May 1956 issue of Harley-Davidson's *The Enthusiast* magazine, for a story titled "Who Is Elvis Presley?" It's also the motorcycle depicted on the cover of Presley's *Return of the Rocker* compilation album.

Elvis rode the KH until November of 1956, when he upgraded to a 1957 Harley-Davidson FLH. He sold the KH to his riding buddy Fleming Horne, who eventually sold the bike—along with complete documentation, including the bill of sale and registration paperwork, all signed by Presley—to Harley-Davidson in 1995. It has been the centerpiece of the Harley-Davidson Museum's Pop Culture exhibit since the museum opened in 2008.

The K-series was Harley-Davidson's first attempt at a modern, sporty motorcycle to compete with lightweight British machines that were taking over the American market in the early 1950s. Harley-Davidson initially ignored this British invasion and instead concentrated on making its Big Twin lineup quieter, more reliable, and easier to maintain. But by 1951, when Harley-Davidson sales dropped to just fifteen thousand units and Norton, Triumph, and BSA combined sold roughly twice that number in the United States, the Motor Company could no longer afford not to pay attention to the midsized market segment.

Harley-Davidson's first volley in this brewing performance war was the 1952 Model K, a semi-sporty machine that was nonetheless significantly smaller, lighter, more agile, and more affordable than any of the Motor Company's Big Twins. Power came from a 45-cubic-inch flathead engine with an integrated (unit-construction) four-speed, foot-shift transmission, and suspension was composed of hydraulic components front and rear. Excepting the aged flathead engine design, the Model K was an otherwise modern and up-to-date motorcycle.

The K-model was the sportiest Harley-Davidson ever built, but it was still no match for the lighter, faster British twins—especially not after British manufacturers upsized their 500s to 650cc and

then added features such as dual carbs and more compression. Not even a displacement increase from 45 to 55 cubic inches in 1954 (to create the KH model) could put the Harley-Davidson in the same league. The Motor Company needed to get serious, and it finally did in 1957 by replacing the outdated flathead top end with all-new pushrod OHV cylinders to create the very first Sportster model, the Sportster XL. Though Harley-Davidson engineers didn't know it at the time, the Sportster would soon become most successful and longest-lived motorcycle platform in Harley-Davidson history—one that is still going strong some sixty-plus years later, making the Sportster one of the longest continuously produced motorcycle models in the world.

The Sportster looked more like a contemporary sportbike than any Harley-Davidson before, and capable of producing 32 horsepower at 4,200 rpm (both impressive numbers at that time), the big-bore, short-stroke Sportster performed like one too. Response in the marketplace was beyond enthusiastic—the new Sportster was a smash hit, successfully drawing many riders away from British bikes and back to American iron. The new "Ironhead" OHV engine—so called because the cylinders and heads both were made from cast iron—was such an improvement over the outdated flathead that by 1958 all the K-bikes were discontinued. At the same time, the XL lineup expanded rapidly to include the stripped-down XLH high-compression version, plus the XLCH (racing) version.

By 1960, Sportster production had increased to 2,765 units, a 40-percent increase over 1957. By 1967, Sportster production grew to 4,500 units—second only to the top-of-the-line Electra-Glide—and by 1970, the Sportster was Harley-Davidson's top-selling model at 8,560 units, out-pacing the Electra-Glide by nearly 1,000 units.

The Sportster's impact on the Harley-Davidson Motor Company—and on global motorcycle culture—can hardly be overstated. No motorcycle in Harley-Davidson's history has ever been more versatile, if not successful. Sportsters have been adapted to—and have succeeded at—nearly every form of motorcycle racing, from hillclimbing to drag racing to land-speed racing to flat-track and everything else. A true chameleon, the Sportster can be the ultimate streetfighter or the mildest entry-level bike—like in the mid-1980s, when the 883 Sportster was priced below $4,000 to bring more consumers to the Harley-Davidson brand, attracting a huge number of first-time riders to motorcycling—many of them women. The Sportster is an amazing success story, and, sixty years later, it is still the definition of cool. Elvis very well might have been the first to notice this fact, but he certainly wasn't the last.

The original "studio action" shot of the 1958 XLCH, the racing version of the Sportster platform.

26

CYCLE CHAMP JACKET

Is there any motorcycle accessory more iconic than the black leather biker jacket? It's a timeless style that has long since transcended motorcycling to become one of pop culture's most enduring symbols of rebellion, adopted by every counterculture from rockers to punks to metalheads to hip-hop stars and beyond. Today, you are equally likely see a black leather jacket on a Hollywood red carpet or a Paris fashion runway or in your local hipster coffee shop—and it looks equally cool in each setting. Even if you aren't brave enough to ride a Harley-Davidson motorcycle, a black leather motorcycle jacket lets you look the part.

To everyone from rebel outsiders to fashion insiders, the black leather motorcycle jacket is now sartorial shorthand for cool. But this wasn't always the case. The original leather motorcycle jackets were designed for function first, fabricated from heavy-duty leather that provided protection from both abrasion and from the elements too.

Leather comes in many colors, of course, but black soon became the color of choice for motorcyclists. Remember, in the pre-Knucklehead days, all motorcycles used total-loss oiling systems. Where did all that excess oil go? Usually, it sprayed all over the rider, so wearing black only made sense. In fact, old timers claim you could once tell Harley-Davidson riders from Indian riders

just by looking at the back of their jackets—the oil flung from the chains was on the left for Harley-Davidson riders, and the right for Indians.

The leather jacket-rebellious outsider connection first emerged with returning World War II vets who formed the first outlaw motorcycle clubs. They often could be seen racing around town on Army-surplus WLA bobbers, wearing Army-surplus leather bomber jackets. But it was the actor Marlon Brando, playing the role of Johnny Strabler, who cemented the image of the black leather jacket as the official uniform of rebel outcasts everywhere when he roared onto the scene during the opening credits of the 1953 film *The Wild One*, unforgettably adorned in a jet-black Schott Perfecto "One Star" jacket.

"Hey Johnny, what are you rebelling against?" Mildred, the girl next door, asks Brando "Whadda you got?" Brando snaps back, flashing his signature sneer. Wrapped in leather, and cool as ice.

Harley-Davidson debuted its own version of the iconic black motorcycle jacket in 1954 when it introduced the now-classic

Cycle Champ jacket, complete with stylish features including an attached belt and a detachable fur collar. (The Motor Company also debuted a complementary Cycle Queen jacket that same year, designed just for female riders.)

Harley-Davidson continued to manufacture the Cycle Champ for many decades, with styling that evolved to keep up with changing fashions and changing times. Numerous versions are displayed in the museum collection, including one from the mid-1970s with an extended back panel for extra support, inspired by early kidney belts. There's even a low-cost nylon version on display—the Titan Cycle Champ—that was produced for a short period during the 1970s.

Even though the black leather motorcycle jacket was once derided as "a symbol of delinquency" preferred by a certain group of "youngsters who go about dressed as motorcyclists [but] don't even own one"—as Harley-Davidson president William H. Davidson noted in a 1960 statement—it has since become a revered symbol of style and individuality, and one that's all but inseparable from Harley-Davidson's hard-earned image of rebellious cool.

27

TOPPER STEREOSCOPE

Motor scooters have to be counted among the very first of countless baby boomer-driven consumer crazes, alongside color television, hula hoops, and Frisbees. In the late 1950s, it seemed like almost every teenager in America had access to a cheap and easy-to-use scooter that seemed purpose-built for a quick ride down to the local department store to pick up the latest Elvis record, or a goofy mouse-ear hat to wear while watching "The Mickey Mouse Club."

Cushman scooters, made in Lincoln, Nebraska, were the most popular early models, selling over fifteen thousand units in 1958 alone—not including the rebranded versions sold through Sears department stores under the Allstate name.

Harley-Davidson officially entered this overheated scooter market in 1960 when it released the Topper, a simple step-through machine with a boxy fiberglass body, powered by a pull-start, two-stroke single and rolling on solid-disc wheels. A low center of gravity, no-shift "scootaway" drive, and fuel economy in the

range of 100 miles per gallon made the Topper particularly appealing to young consumers at a time when the youth market was emerging as a key consumer category. An influential 1958 story in *Life* magazine titled "4,000,000 a Year Make Millions in Business" declared these kids a "built-in recession cure." This was a demographic the Motor Company couldn't afford to ignore.

To better connect with these kids, Harley-Davidson experimented with all manner of new and innovative advertising techniques targeted directly at younger consumers—like the stereoscope

box pictured here. A stereoscope is a simple device that presents a pair of separate images—left-eye and right-eye views of the same scene—combined in a single three-dimensional image. Stereoscopes, more commonly associated with the brand name View-Master, were hugely popular with kids in the '50s and '60s, and presenting the Topper product in this trendy format was an inspired way to connect with the youth market. Harley-Davidson's "Man About the World" stereoscope viewer from 1960 featured a beach scene with copy marketing the Topper scooter as a hip leisure machine.

Harley-Davidson made significant use of other relevant advertising methods too, including lifestyle marketing and especially the use of celebrity endorsers. Early magazine ads for the Topper prominently featured actor Edd "Kookie" Byrnes

from the wildly popular TV detective series *77 Sunset Strip*. One particularly memorable ad headline read "Kookie Lend Me Your Topper"—a play on the novelty hit song "Kookie, Kookie (Lend Me Your Comb)," performed by Byrnes and Connie Stevens.

Like so many youth trends of the time, the scooter fad faded as fast as it appeared. Despite these innovative advertising strategies, Harley-Davidson's Topper enjoyed only moderate sales success until it was eventually discontinued after 1965. There was, however, one completely unanticipated side effect of this boom-and-bust scooter trend that had an absolutely profound impact on the future of the Harley-Davidson Motor Company. That was the hiring of a young William G. Davidson—grandson of William A. Davidson, one of the four founders—now better known to the world simply as "Willie G."

FOR PROFIT

FOR FUN

WILLIAM G. DAVIDSON

HARLEY-DAVIDSON APPOINTS THIRD GENERATION DAVIDSON DIRECTOR OF STYLING

The Harley-Davidson Motor Co. has appointed a new Director of Styling. He is William G. Davidson, 29, a grandson of Wm. A. Davidson, one of the founders of the Company, and the son of Wm. H. Davidson, the firm's president. As Director of Styling, Davidson will supervise the styling of all Harley-Davidson motorcycles, motor scooters, golf cars and accessories.

Davidson has had design experience with the Continental Division of the Ford Motor Co.; the Packaging Design Studio of Milprint Inc. in Milwaukee, Wisconsin; and, most recently, with the internationally famous design organization, Brooks Stevens Associates, also located in Milwaukee. He attended the University of Wisconsin in Madison and, later, the Art Center School in Los Angeles, California, graduating in 1957 with a Bachelor of Professional Arts degree.

Married and the father of two boys and a girl, Davidson is an avid motorcycle enthusiast and has been riding regularly since he was 16. He is a life member of the American Motorcycle Association, attends as many races as he can, and is an experienced enduro rider.

Members of the Lebanon Valley Motorcycle Club, Lebanon, Pa., once again participated in the annual March of Dimes Campaign. This is the third year in succession that the Club served by distributing dimes containers to business places throughout the city. This photo was taken by the local television station for use on local news shows and for March of Dimes publicity. Members shown, *left to right, front row,* are: Leon Burkholder, Pete Morris, Henrietta Steiner—club secretary and Richard Kohr. *Back row,* Bruce Steiner, Joseph White, Marion White—club treasurer and Richard Steiner—club vice president.

Shown in their classroom are the dealers and mechanics who attended the Harley-Davidson Service School from January 28 through February 9, 1963. They are:

First row, left to right—Forrest H. Melick, Newark, Ohio; Alton B. McGlocklin, Chattanooga, Tennessee; James A. Hollingsworth, St. Augustine, Florida; Harold C. Thomas, Jr., St. Augustine, Florida; and Arthur D. Bernheisel, Belmont, California.

Second row, left to right—George F. Shaffer, Greensboro, Maryland; Vern W. Fuller, Lincoln, Nebraska; James B. Johnson, Columbia, Missouri; Jack A. Moss, Boston, Massachusetts; and Edward A. Turner, Buffalo, New York.

Third row, left to right—Don D. Smith, Inglewood, California; Haldon H. Hartman, Douglas, Arizona; Charles F. Popovich, Alton, Illinois; Wendell A. Smith, Milwaukee, Wisconsin; and Elmer C. Chestelson, Cornell, Iowa.

Fourth row, left to right—Howard W. Belmont, St. Paul, Minnesota; David H. Warren, Jr., Roanoke, Virginia; Carl J. Hyson, Jr., West Bridgewater, Massachusetts; Robert A. Mauriello, Bloomfield, New Jersey; and Wayne E. Cook, Petersburg, Virginia.

Fifth row, left to right—Lesley Ford and Raymond Meinnert, both from Milwaukee, Wisconsin.

Standing in the rear are, left to right, instructors Richard C. Marshall, John Nowak, Robert Jameson, Sidney Soiney, George Klenzendorf and Albert Henrich, and Harley-Davidson's Service Manager Joseph Ryan.

Rider Hand Book

HARLEY-DAVIDSON

Motor Scooter

It was the early 1960s and Willie G, recently graduated from Art Center College of Design in Pasadena, California, was employed as a junior designer at Brooks Stevens Design—a world-class industrial design firm known for shaping everything from home appliances to automobiles to passenger trains. As one of five designers in Brooks Stevens' Transportation and Product Design group, a young Willie G was tasked with creating everything from entertainment centers to outboard motors to motor scooters, the latter for one of Brooks Stevens Design's biggest clients—Cushman.

One day Willie G was having lunch with his father William H. Davidson—then the president of Harley-Davidson—when the discussion naturally turned to the problematic idea of the younger Davidson designing products that directly competed with one of the elder Davidson's key new-product initiatives. The inevitable output of this discussion was the birth of a plan for Willie G to join Harley-Davidson to create the firm's first Styling Department, a division he would ultimately lead for the entire forty-nine years he officially worked at the Motor Company.

Before Willie G's arrival, design at Harley-Davidson was mostly a side effect of engineering. In those days, a good design was one that worked well and was easy to manufacture. Beauty and form were secondary concerns, if that. But by the time the '60s rolled around, with a rapidly expanding portfolio of products that included lightweight motorcycles, scooters, boats, and even golf carts, the elder Davidson knew it was past time for Harley-Davidson to establish an in-house design department in order to stay competitive. And he was certain that his young son, having

trained at one of the best design schools in the world and worked alongside a legendary industrial design pioneer, was the right person to direct this new department.

Willie G officially joined the family business in 1963, and his relatives in charge showed no evidence of favoritism—his first job was designing interiors for the Tomahawk boats that Harley-Davidson manufactured during the 1960s. Fiberglass designs, from golf car bodies to motorcycle saddlebags, were a primary focus during Willie G's first years at the company.

The job wasn't always easy for Willie G. Many of his early ideas were met with resistance from conservative upper management, who considered his custom culture-influenced designs radical and unpractical, but market success eventually won him approval. Willie G was promoted to vice president of styling in 1969, and under his leadership, he brought a unified aesthetic to the look and feel of all Harley-Davidson products.

Even after his official retirement in 2012, when he assumed the position of chief styling officer emeritus, Willie G remains the most recognizable figure associated with the Harley-Davidson brand, hardly ever seen without his trademark felt beret and aviator-style eyeglasses. In the intervening five decades, he played a key role in defining many motorcycle industry trends. He effectively invented the factory custom when he created the FX Super Glide in 1971, and he hasn't looked back since. But who would have ever thought that Willie G, a character so utterly synonymous with macho and masculine Big Twin American motorcycles, earned his design chops styling pull-start, step-through scooters?

28

KING KONG

Custom motorcycle culture really took off during the 1960s. Custom motorcycles were nothing new, of course—riders had been modifying their bikes since the very dawn of the sport—but prior to that time, most modifications were made in the service of better performance or improved functionality.

But starting in the '60s, individuality, self-expression, and aesthetics became a driving force, if not the driving force. Inspired by the "kustom kulture" typified by hot rod builders such as Ed "Big Daddy" Roth and the George Barris, along with visual artists such as Von Dutch and Robert Williams, the custom motorcycle trend exploded with the advent of the chopper. Featuring exaggerated styling characterized by raked-out forks, oversized wheels, sculpted bodywork, and psychedelic paint, the chopper was the antithesis of the built-for-speed bobber—and it changed custom motorcycles forever.

Numerous examples of custom motorcycles are featured in the Harley-Davidson Museum collection, ranging from the sublime to the ridiculous, but none are more outrageous than this radical,

dual-engine contraption nicknamed *King Kong*. Built by Felix Predko, a Harley-Davidson mechanic and amateur metalsmith from Windber, Pennsylvania, *King Kong* is a particular type of mechanical folk art handcrafted especially to satisfy Predko's uniquely personal taste.

Originally constructed in 1953 (but continuously tweaked for the next four decades), *King Kong* merges two FL frames and two Knucklehead engines into a single, massive, 13-foot-long, highway cruiser. The longer you study *King Kong*, taking in odd details such as the dual handlebars, the cartoonishly extended fenders, and the on-board stereo, the more impressive—and inexplicable—it all becomes.

Predko originally conceived of the machine as a clever way to advertise his independent shop, Felix's H-D Sales and Service. He actually began his career as a factory-certified mechanic at a franchised dealership (Zepka Harley-Davidson), but that didn't last long. Predko wasn't one for doing things by the book. His instructor's record card from the Harley-Davidson Service School (which is also on display at the museum, dating from 1948) reflected more than a few negative comments. An independent custom shop suited Predko much better.

Predko considered himself an iron artist, and *King Kong* is a visual record of both his imagination and his mechanical ingenuity. Exaggerated aluminum bodywork wraps both ends of *King Kong*, incorporating details such as taillights taken from a 1959 Cadillac and a pair of scuba tanks adapted to supply compressed air to the trio of freight-train horns. Predko didn't restrict his metalworking skills to his motorcycle. He also accentuated his riding gear—including a modified batter's helmet—with handcrafted metal wrist cuffs, belts, and boot gaiters, all featuring Predko's signature hand-punched border.

"The flashier, the better" is how Predko's grandson, Brian DiNinno, describes the style. In addition to many of Predko's decorative riding accessories, the museum collection also displays an assortment of Predko's metal punches and a small hammer that he used to create his art.

King Kong isn't the only piece of rolling folk art on display at the Harley-Davidson Museum. Just a few yards away stands the 1973 FLH "Rhinestone-Glide," created by Russ Townsend as a form of therapy as he recovered from an accident. Covered with tens of thousands of red, white, and blue rhinestones—plus a few dozen yards of Trimbrite pinstriping tape, a couple hundred metal studs, and enough accessory lights to require an extra alternator—you can see Townsend's creation coming from miles away. A variety of beads, metal studs, and other accessories, along with the jeweler's setting tool used by Townsend to give the bike its "sparkling" personality, are displayed alongside the glittering machine.

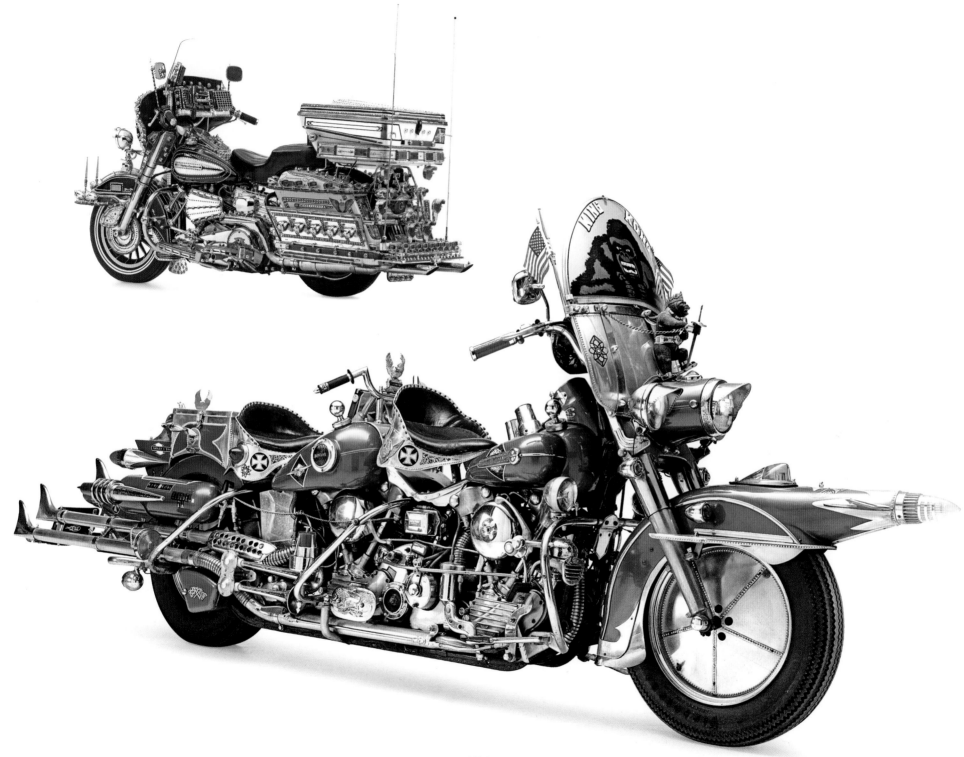

29

DICK O'BRIEN (LEFT), JAY SPRINGSTEEN (SECOND FROM LEFT), AND BILL WERNER (RIGHT) CELEBRATE ONE OF THE FORTY-THREE AMA NATIONAL WINS THEY EARNED TOGETHER WITH THE XR-750.

XR-750

Harley-Davidson's flathead-powered KR racers, originally released in 1952, were still winning national championships well into the 1960s—long after any bike that relied on such outdated engine technology should have remained relevant. This disproportionate success was mostly due to the AMA's so-called "equivalency" rule that favored America's last remaining manufacturer by allowing flathead engines a 250cc displacement advantage compared to overhead-valve engines, which were limited to just 500cc. By the late 1960s, however, the AMA was feeling increased pressure from British and Japanese motorcycle manufacturers—which had long since abandoned flathead technology in favor of more modern designs—to rewrite the Class C racing rules and undo what many considered an advantage that only benefitted Harley-Davidson.

So in 1969, the AMA instituted simplified Class C racing rules that eliminated the equivalency clause, instituting a 750cc displacement limit for all racing engines regardless of valve arrangement *or* cylinder count. The playing field had been leveled—now Harley-Davidson had to come up with a new racing motorcycle design, and quick.

This new ruling couldn't have come at a worse time. Harley-Davidson was in deep financial trouble in 1969, and midway through that year, American Machine Foundry (AMF), a company better known for making bowling equipment, acquired the Motor Company. AMF had its hands full restructuring labor

and production, and the last thing company executives were worried about was flat-track racing. Harley-Davidson racers needed a hero, someone with the exact right combination of imagination and resourcefulness to create something from nothing. That hero was Dick O'Brien.

Wickedly smart and fiercely determined, O'Brien—OB to his friends—was a highly successful tuner and racer in Orlando, Florida, when he was handpicked by Hank Syvertsen to take over the racing department in 1957. OB's early years were characterized by massive success. Despite heavy competition from British brands, OB and his riders won the AMA Grand National Championship nine out of ten years between 1957 to 1966. Then Triumph won the title in 1967 and '68, and the writing was on the wall. New rules for 1969 only sealed the KR's fate. The Motor Company desperately needed a new racing motorcycle, and they needed to do it on the cheap.

Scrounging around the Juneau Avenue race shop, OB found a possible solution in the Sportster XLR—the race-only version of the OHV Sportster that was originally released in 1958. Beginning with the XLR's basic Ironhead V-twin, OB installed shorter-stroke flywheels to reduce displacement from 883cc to 750cc (to comply with AMA rules) and then added even hotter cams to further boost performance. This hastily redesigned racing engine was dropped into a modified KR chassis and topped with revised fiberglass bodywork to create the XR-750—Harley-Davidson's newest race-ready dirt tracker.

Developed in just over four months, the XR-750 debuted to the public in February 1970 at the Houston Astrodome. By all accounts, the XR-750 was a complete failure. Not only was the Ironhead XR-750 slow, it was very unreliable too—earning the unfortunate nickname "waffle iron" for its extreme tendency to overheat, especially on the longer, more grueling miles. Both

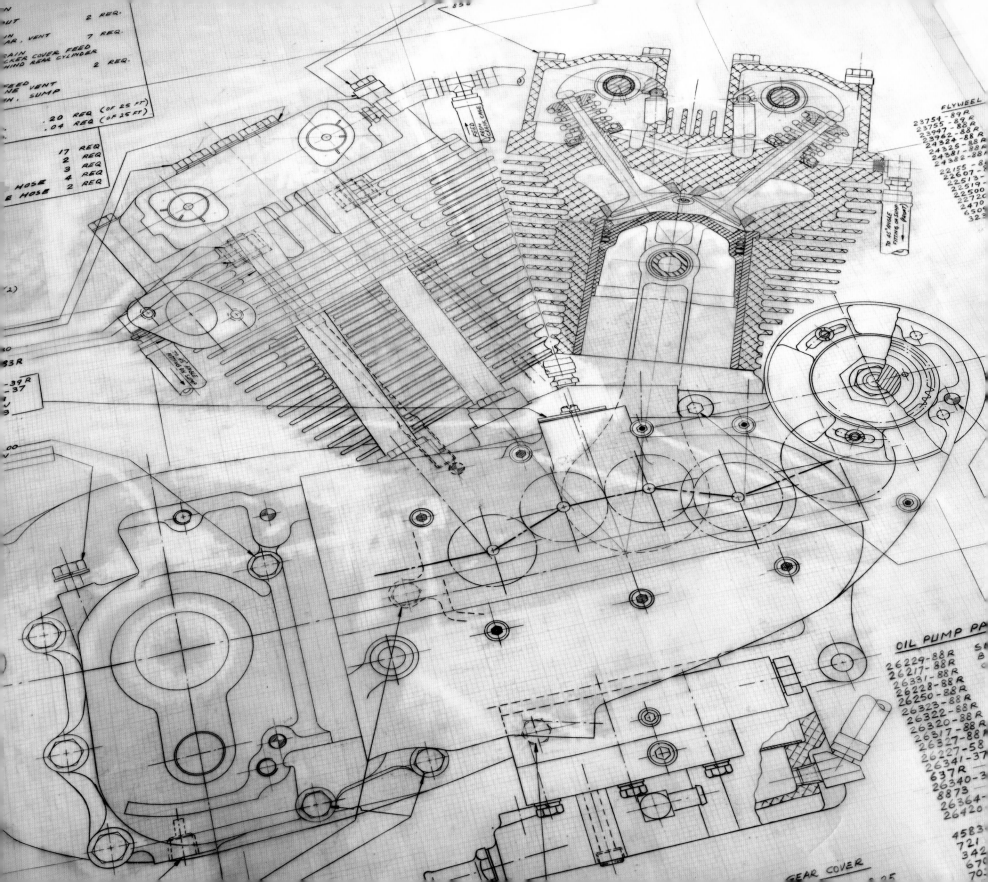

problems could be traced directly to the outdated cast-iron cylinder heads and barrels that were quick to heat up and slow to cool down. The XR-750 did win one race that first year—at Ascot with Mert Lawwill—but mostly they just melted down. Harley-Davidson built two hundred XR-750s, as required by AMA homologation rules, but factory records show only half that number was actually sold—the rest were either dismantled or destroyed.

The tale of the XR-750 is actually the tale of two bikes. The first bike is the Iron XR, which disappeared almost as fast as it appeared; the second bike is the Alloy XR, which went on to become perhaps the greatest racing motorcycle of all time. OB was finally able to squeeze some development dollars out of AMF in advance of the 1972 racing season, and he used that money to redesign the XR-750 engine from the top-down with lighter and better-cooling aluminum cylinder heads and barrels, as well as a new dual-carburetor setup—good for nearly 80 horsepower, a number that matched the best British bikes.

The new engine was designed by Peter Zylstra, a young Dutch engineer with international road-racing experience who had joined the Harley-Davidson engineering department in 1969. Zylstra also designed a new and lighter chassis to carry the alloy XR engine, cutting dry weight to below 300 pounds—another very competitive figure. For the first time in many, many years, Harley-Davidson racers had an absolutely up-to-date racing platform.

Unlike the Iron XR that preceded it, the Alloy XR was immediately successful. California rider Mark Brelsford won the 1972 AMA Grand National Championship aboard the XR-750, kicking off an unprecedented era of Harley-Davidson dirt-track dominance. Harley-Davidson XR-750-mounted riders went on to win thirty-seven of forty-four AMA flat-track championships from 1972 to

2015—more wins than any bike in AMA racing history, and quite likely more wins than any other bike in motorcycle racing history period, regardless of surface or series.

Many riders achieved success on XR-750s, but two in particular—Jay Springsteen and Scott Parker—are especially linked to that machine. Springsteen earned the AMA Rookie of the Year Award in 1975 before winning three consecutive AMA Grand National Championships starting in 1976, all riding for the Harley-Davidson factory team. Born in Flint, Michigan, "Springer," as his fans know him, raced in a record 398 AMA nationals and won a total of forty-three—all partnered with Harley-Davidson tuner Bill Werner. Together, they had one of the longest-lived and most successful relationships in the history of the sport.

Scott Parker, a nine-time AMA Grand National Champion, holds the all-time record of ninety-four Grand National Championship race wins. Also hailing from Flint, Michigan, Parker was the youngest rider ever to win an AMA Grand National Series race, at age seventeen. Parker won his first GNC in 1988 and never looked back, winning four consecutive years to match H-D rider Carroll Resweber's record. Then, with a run that started in 1994, Parker became the first rider in history to win five straight AMA Grand National Championships—establishing a career record that very well might never be bested.

Harley-Davidson built its last complete XR-750 in 1980—making this decades-long winning streak all the more remarkable. There are no reliable production records—and many XR-750s were known to be purposefully destroyed by the factory for tax accounting reasons—but it's thought that only around five hundred complete XR-750s were ever built. After that final 1980 production run, only the XR-750 engine was offered for sale, with the customer choosing an aftermarket frame to construct a complete bike.

DICK O'BRIEN'S SUPERFLOW
110 FLOWBENCH. MANY
CHAMPIONSHIP-WINNING RACE
MOTORS WERE BORN RIGHT HERE.

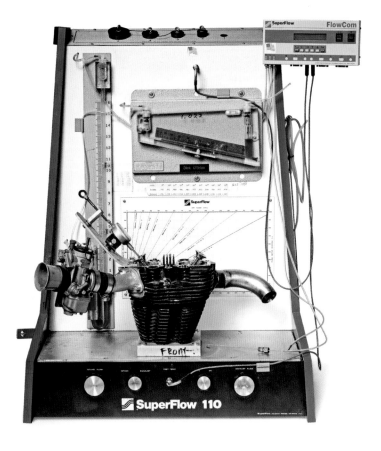

Harley-Davidson was painfully slow to respond to demand for a street-legal XR-750, finally releasing the XR-1000 in 1983. Essentially, a standard Sportster XL fit with XR-750 heads, dual carbs, and high-mounted race-type exhaust, the XR-1000 sold for nearly twice the price of the standard XL. Predictably, it was a poor seller and it was discontinued after just two years—of course, it is highly collectable now. Somewhat more successful was the XR-1200 that was released in 2008 (or 2009, if you lived in the United States). More versatile than the XR-1000 and more

powerful too, thanks to engine technology borrowed from the Buell sportbikes, the 90-horsepower XR-1200 even spawned a popular AMA spec roadracing series that ran for five years.

The story of the Harley-Davidson XR-750 is the story of a purely American motorcycle built to dominate a purely American sport. This is undoubtedly the most successful racing motorcycle ever built—one that utterly dominated dirt-track racing for more than four decades, and one that is still winning national events right up to the present day.

30

WORLD CHAMPIONSHIP ROADRACING

Harley-Davidson purchased a 50-percent share of Italian aircraft manufacturer Aermacchi's motorcycle division in 1960. The decision made perfect sense. Modern lightweight motorcycles made in Britain, Europe, and especially Japan were upending the American motorcycle market, and Harley-Davidson couldn't compete with its lineup of Hummers and other outdated, low-tech two-strokes. The Aermacchi arrangement allowed Harley-Davidson to replace its lightweight lineup entirely with more fashionable and functional Aermacchi products, including a popular four-stroke single available in both 250cc and 350cc variants that was rebadged as the Harley-Davidson Sprint.

The Aermacchi partnership also opened another less obvious opportunity for Harley-Davidson, in the realm of World Championship roadracing. Harley-Davidson was heavily involved in roadracing in America, of course, but the firm had never consistently competed on the world stage. The early '70s, however, were a time of huge transition in roadracing, when light, cheap, and fast two-stroke racers from Yamaha (and other Japanese manufacturers) revolutionized the sport. Aermacchi wanted to play along, so chief designer William Soncini created the RR-250—which actually borrowed some engine internals from the Yamaha TD to save development and manufacturing costs—to create Harley-Davidson's own light, cheap, and very fast two-stroke roadracing platform.

The RR-250 launched in 1971, but the platform didn't really begin to prove its potential until 1972. That year, Harley-Davidson factory rider Renzo Pasolini won three Grands Prix (and the Italian national championship) on the way to a second-place finish in the 250GP World Championship and third in the 350GP class (the latter on a bored-and-stroked RR-250). Hopes were high for a world title in 1973, when the veteran Pasolini—then leading the 250GP World Championship—was killed in a horrific racing accident at the Italian GP along with then-reigning 250GP World Champion Jarno Saarinen, in a day now remembered as "Black Sunday."

That's when an unassuming Italian racer named Walter Villa was hired to assume the role of Harley-Davidson's lead rider for the 1974 season—the same year that Harley-Davidson purchased all remaining shares of Aermacchi's motorcycle division.

Over the winter of 1973 and 1974, Aermacchi chief engineer Dr. Sandro Colombo made huge progress in developing the RR-250. Colombo's major improvement was the adaptation of liquid cooling, which allowed the already-fast parallel twin—capable of producing 49 horsepower in air-cooled form—to better maintain its composure over long GP race distances. Villa made the most of these advancements, winning that year's early-season Italian Grand Prix with an incredible forty-four-second lead over the next closest competitor.

Quiet and workmanlike off the bike but ruthless in the saddle, Villa rode the RR-250 for all it was worth over the length of the 1974 season, going on to win three more rounds at Brno (Czechoslovakia), Imatra (Finland), and Assen (Netherlands). This performance was good enough to earn Harley-Davidson its first Grand Prix World Championship and the first 250GP World Championship in four years to go to someone besides a Yamaha rider, to shatter that brand's four-year streak.

It turns out this was the beginning of a Harley-Davidson winning streak, when Villa returned to take victories at five rounds during the 1975 season—in Spain, Germany, Italy, Holland, and Sweden—to win the 250GP championship for a second year in a row. Villa was described in period literature as an unlikely champion—"short, chunky and unusually boyish," in an era typified by playboys such as Giacomo Agostini, Johnny Cecotto, and Barry Sheene—but when the helmets were on, Villa had no equal. In 1976, the quiet racer from Varese accomplished a feat that has been matched by precious few racers, winning dual world championships in both the 250cc (his third in a row) and 350cc classes. He cinched that year's 250 championship at Brno, leading from flag-to-flag, and locked up the 350 championship the next weekend at Nürburgring in Germany—the first time since 1967 that a double championship was won.

31

FXB STURGIS

The best ideas are often born from a simple sketch. The physical act of putting pen to paper and drawing lines fires different neural circuits in the brain and allows you to see familiar things in new and original ways—triggering your imagination and unleashing your most creative impulses. Sketching is the easiest and fastest way to get an idea out of your head and in front of your eyes, where you can begin to really see the opportunities for innovation and improvement.

Harley-Davidson Chief Styling Officer Willie G. Davidson well understood the power of a good sketch to aid the creative process, and he frequently worked out the finer points of his designs using a pen and whatever scratch paper he had on-hand—in this case, an everyday brown paper bag. The year was 1979, and Willie G was riding a belt-drive prototype back to Milwaukee after the annual rally at Sturgis, South Dakota, when the inspiration to draw took over. He pulled off the road and jotted down a few notes— drag handlebars; extended forks; a racy, 2-into-1 exhaust; mag wheels; and highway pegs—on a scrap of brown paper bag. These

off-the-cuff ideas eventually shaped the limited-edition 1980 FXB Sturgis motorcycle—one of the most iconic and influential motorcycle designs of Harley-Davidson's modern era.

Willie G always found inspiration outside of the design lab—often on the open road. His first truly groundbreaking design, the 1971 FX Super Glide, was heavily influenced by the custom choppers he saw plying the streets of Southern California. The Super Glide combined Harley-Davidson's Big Twin chassis and Shovelhead engine with the narrower, lighter front end from the Sportster

WILLIE G'S STURGIS NOTES
HANDWRITTEN ON A PAPER BAG.

A CONTACT SHEET OF
PROMOTIONAL PHOTOS TO
SUPPORT THE LAUNCH OF THE
1971 FX SUPER GLIDE.

model, then covered it all in a one-piece, fiberglass "boat-tail" tail section finished with "Sparkling America" paint that was clearly a nod to Captain America chopper from the film *Easy Rider*. Just like that, Willie G created the factory-custom concept that still drives Harley-Davidson's design philosophy almost fifty years later.

The Super Glide represented a significant risk for the Motor Company. For most of the 1960s, Harley-Davidson turned its back on the outlaw motorcycle community and the chopper-style bikes these trend-setting riders preferred, instead concentrating corporate attention on full-dress touring motorcycles and squeaky-clean lightweight products pitched to respectable, upstanding citizens. But the advent of the Super Glide—and the tacit acknowledgment of the chopper culture that inspired that design—was a huge departure for the normally conservative Harley-Davidson Motor Company. Luckily, the model was well received in the marketplace, even if many buyers immediately replaced the ungainly boat tail with a standard Sportster rear fender. It instantly formed a bridge between Harley-Davidson

THE LOW RIDER. YOU DON'T GET ON IT. YOU GET IN IT.

Those who take on this one, have to be pure biker.

They'll get in the lowest Harley-Davidson motorcycle there's ever been. With a ground to seat height fully two-inches lower than the lowest of the Super Bikes, our own Super Glide. They'll have beneath them a bull of a hybrid: With extended forks and drag style handlebars with

3½" risers above a Sportster style front end, 1200 cc's of pure Super Glide power, and need-less to say, the famous Harley-Davidson sound of thunder rumbling through a tunnel.

They'll have twin, fat bob gas tanks surrounding the tach and speedometer that's mounted between them on the console. Dual front disc brakes.

And for looks, black wrinkle crankcases, black cylinders and heads with polished fins and silver finished fork sliders, with custom clutch cover and fender supports.

There will be just one color (silver), and the

fat bob gas tanks will be honored by a 1930-style Harley-Davidson decal.

As you can see, this is one motorcycle the town librarian won't take to the church social.

Other than offering that generality, we refuse to speculate,

Help keep insurance costs down. Lock your bike.

We believe in safety first. Before you start out, light your lights, put on your h

and the youth culture that the Motor Company—and all those many Harley-Davidson dealers—needed so desperately to connect with in order to insure its future survival.

Willie G's next major design milestone was the FXS Low Rider—essentially a lowered and raked Super Glide—which was released to the public in 1977. Inspired once again by custom motorcycle trends, the aptly named Low Rider featured a seat that skimmed just 27 inches above the pavement, creating a long-and-low profile that still looks radical even today. The aforementioned Sturgis edition was a Low Rider variant, as was the first Wide Glide model—also released in 1980—which substituted apehanger handlebars, a stepped seat, staggered dual pipes, and flamed paint to create an even wilder factory-chopper look. These were the bikes that set the direction for the next for the next three decades of Harley-Davidson style.

Though some critics contend that Harley-Davidson lost its way under AMF ownership in the 1970s, so many seminal motorcycles from that period suggest otherwise. Willie G's unwavering style leadership—and his uncanny ability to create something from nothing by endlessly recombining existing parts in new and novel ways—almost single-handedly kept Harley-Davidson afloat through this challenging time. Each of these new models attracted more and more new customers, expanding Harley-Davidson's market share. More importantly, such iconic, on-trend designs shaped the future of the entire motorcycle industry. Harley-Davidson's Dyna motorcycle family, introduced in 1991, traces its ancestry directly to the Low Rider—as do so many Japanese (and European) cruiser platforms, which are essentially Harley-Davidson knockoffs. Once again, Harley-Davidson was the company that every other motorcycle manufacturer wanted to emulate.

32

DRONE ROCKET ENGINE

This is probably the single most surprising—or remarkable, or unexpected, or baffling—object in the entire Harley-Davidson Museum Collection. Anyone can understand the electric bike, and the reverse trike, and the snowmobiles, and speedboats, and even the golf carts . . . but a Harley-Davidson rocket engine? For real?

Yes, Harley-Davidson really did build a rocket engine—or, more precisely, more than five thousand individual rocket engines, over a thirty-year timespan, beginning in the 1960s—for use powering US Navy target drones. Originally designed by Rocketdyne, a Canoga Park, California-based rocket engine design company, Harley-Davidson manufactured the LR-64 rocket engine in its York plant to power the AQM-37 Jayhawk Supersonic target drones employed specifically to simulate inbound ICBMs (inter-continental ballistic missiles) for US Navy "shoot-down" exercises. Measuring 21 x 10 x 5 inches, the LR-64 rocket engine was used by the US military to simulate different missile attacks. Certain models were even fitted with two-stage parachutes so they could be recovered—in the event that they were not shot down— and reused after certain exercises.

Each of these compact rocket engines was installed in a 14-foot-long fuselage, with a 3-foot, 4-inch wingspan and a gross weight of 620 pounds. These rocket engines used storable liquid propellants, which meant they had the advantage of not needing to be fueled before flight. The downside to storable propellants is that they are highly toxic and corrosive—not to mention that these propellants could spontaneously ignite when mixed—making the long-term survival of these rockets even more tenuous. The Motor Company has held military contracts dating back to the teens, and these government contracts often helped to support and stabilize Motor Company business during challenging market times. Perhaps in a few years, when certain documents are unclassified, we'll find out what military programs—if any—the Harley-Davidson Motor Company might be involved with today.

33

PROJECT NOVA

What if?

Pause and ponder that question for a moment. What if Harley-Davidson—a company overwhelmingly associated with nostalgia, heritage, and a respectful deference to tradition—had at one point embraced modernity instead? It's hard not to wonder how the story we tell about Harley-Davidson might be different today if management had at one point thrown tradition aside in favor of blazing boldly forward into a future unknown. Harley-Davidson's mostly forgotten Nova development project, begun in 1976, offers one potential answer to that question—and a fascinating glimpse into an alternate universe where Harley-Davidson is a technological leader. Consider this chapter a road not taken . . .

Let's start by talking about another manufacturer: Honda's V45 Sabre stunned the motorcycle industry when it was released in 1982. This futuristic machine, powered by a dizzyingly complex, liquid-cooled V-4 engine, confirmed the Japanese manufacturer's reputation as a technological leader. What if we told you Harley-Davidson had designed and built a bike even more technologically advanced than the Sabre and was ready to release it to the public a full year ahead of Honda's schedule?

That bike was the Nova prototype, a machine that predated the revolutionary Honda V-4 by a few years and in many ways was more innovative. Nova was one of the boldest development

projects in all of Harley-Davidson history. Designed in partnership with German automobile manufacturer Porsche, the Nova prototype was powered by a liquid-cooled, dual overhead cam, 60-degree V-4 rated at remarkable 135 horsepower. (Harley-Davidson envisioned multiple versions of the "modular" Nova engine, including a 500cc V-twin, a 1,000cc V-4, and a 1,500cc V-6, but budget pressure resulted in initial development concentrated solely on the V-4.) Porsche handled engine and transmission development; the Motor Company took care of everything else.

The chassis incorporated an underseat radiator and fuel tank, and some versions were equipped with a rim-mounted front brake that predated Buell's Zero Torsional Load (ZTL) design by two decades. Designed specifically to appeal to European and Japanese bike enthusiasts, the Nova was an innovative, compelling machine that certainly would have shifted customers' perceptions of Harley-Davidson to that of an aggressive and daring brand. Unfortunately, the Motor Company killed the expensive and potentially risky project early in 1981, before a single Nova ever went into production.

The Nova wasn't cancelled because it wasn't a good motorcycle. Harley-Davidson completed all validation testing, spending the equivalent of $44 million in today's dollars. More than two dozen operational Nova engines and a dozen completed, running Nova prototype bikes were eventually built, accumulating two thousand hours of dyno and wind-tunnel testing and 100,000 miles on the open road.

Vaughn Beals, then a vice president and soon-to-be company chairman and CEO, was one of the Nova's biggest fans, praising its power and handling. Ultimately, the Nova was casualty of extreme financial insecurity that resulted in the end of the AMF era and the birth of the Evolution engine—setting the stage for three-plus decades of remarkable sales success.

The Nova project was originally concepted during an upper-management retreat in Pinehurst, North Carolina, referred to in Harley-Davidson lore as "the Pinehurst Meeting." The output of this weeklong brainstorm was a two-pronged product strategy that would both update the existing Shovelhead V-twin design—a project that would eventually create the Evo motor, to extend the existing product line—and also develop a new family based on the Nova, to appeal to riders who desired more contemporary performance. Harley-Davidson would become a manufacturer of both traditional and modern motorcycles, filling a white space in the American market and also giving Harley-Davidson increased international appeal.

Even with assistance from Porsche, Harley-Davidson's engineering resources were severely stretched with both programs advancing concurrently. The task of developing the Evo engine—in both Sportster and Big Twin variations—was daunting enough. Developing the Nova at the same time severely overloaded the Motor Company's engineering capacity. Company leadership was forced to choose the path of least resistance, making the difficult decision to scrap Nova and charge forward with Evo development. The rest, as they say, is history.

A PROJECT NOVA-POWERED
ROADRACING PROTOTYPE, FORESHADOWING
THE VR1000 SUPERBIKE THAT DEBUTED
IN 1994.

THE FINAL PROJECT NOVA PROTOTYPE
(LEFT) AND THE 1983 FXRT (RIGHT).
NOTE THE MANY SIMILARITIES—AND
MANY DIFFERENCES.

Project Nova wasn't a complete waste of resources, however. Nova DNA was spliced into multiple future production models. The Nova fairing, for example, developed with prominent air scoops on each side to aid with engine cooling, was adapted almost unchanged to the FXRT touring motorcycle that was released in 1983. Same with the Nova's distinctive, parallelogram-shaped saddlebags—the basic shape of which is still maintained on many Harley-Davidson models today. And of course, the Porsche partnership was revived a few years later to develop the liquid-cooled, 60-degree powertrain at the heart of the VRSC V-Rod model that entered production in 2001.

There's no doubt that beating Honda to market with a high-tech V-4 would have been game-changing for Harley-Davidson, but the firm simply couldn't afford the costs of such a move. The incremental development of the familiar air-cooled V-twin platform to create the Evolution was a more realistic path forward, especially considering the massive downward economic pressure on the Motor Company at the end of the AMF era. That was by necessity the path forward, and the results speak for themselves.

But still, what if?

TRANSFER-OF-OWNERSHIP
CEREMONIAL PEN
JUNE 16, 1981

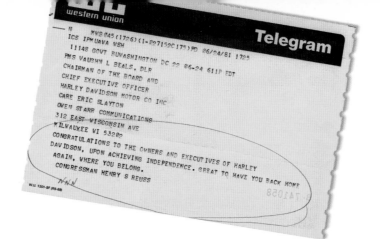

THE BUYBACK

You might rightfully wonder why there is a pen—a Paper Mate Flair felt-tip pen, to be exact—on display at the Harley-Davidson Museum. What on earth does a felt-tip pen have to do with America's greatest motorcycle manufacturer? Believe it or not, this humble felt-tip pen is one of the most significant artifacts in the entire museum collection (no, it's not one of Willie G's design tools . . .). This is the actual pen used to sign the ceremonial transfer-of-ownership documents on June 16, 1981, finalizing the employee buyback of the Motor Company from AMF—a pivotal moment in Harley-Davidson history and one that likely saved the firm from oblivion.

To understand the full magnitude of this moment in Harley-Davidson history, first we have to rewind a few years and understand the story of how Harley-Davidson came to be owned by American Machine Foundry—a company better known then for making bowling balls. The mid-1960s were an extremely challenging time for Harley-Davidson. Faced with a rapidly changing market and increasing competition from Japan, which seemed to produce an endless stream of affordable, accessible, and exciting motorcycles, Harley-Davidson made the decision to go public in 1965, using the cash generated by that initial stock offering to improve both its Milwaukee and Italian (Aermacchi) operations. Difficulties continued, however, and public ownership had opened the door for acquisition by a larger conglomerate—a scenario that terrified company management.

Even though Harley-Davidson was generating cash at the end of the decade, sales were at their lowest point since the Great Depression. It was increasingly harder for a family-owned, single-product company like Harley-Davidson to compete. Soon enough—just as company leaders had feared—Harley-Davidson

faced a hostile takeover attempt from a conglomerate, Bangor Punta. In order to protect itself, Harley-Davidson leadership entered discussions with AMF, a large manufacturer looking to diversify into recreational and leisure products. In January of 1969, Harley-Davidson merged with AMF.

The merger with AMF produced mixed results for Harley-Davidson. Major investments in manufacturing facilities and organization, as well as research and development, improved production and product diversity and allowed the brand to remain competitive. At the same time, however, serious quality-control issues emerged. Many consider the AMF period the darkest in company history, but the real story is more complicated, marking both major triumphs and significant miscalculations.

It was mostly business as usual for the first few years after the merger, until 1971, when AMF transferred production to a

400,000-square-foot facility in York, Pennsylvania. The York factory began making Sportster frames in 1971 (for the 1972 model year) and commenced full motorcycle assembly in 1973. The York factory was much more modern than the tired Milwaukee facilities, but enthusiasts and employees both lamented the move away from Harley-Davidson's hometown.

A 3-mile-long overhead-monorail conveyor was installed at the York plant, with various feeder lines connected to manufacturing departments located throughout the complex. The new plant was so efficient that a complete bike rolled off the assembly line every ninety seconds. Production increased greatly, but more bikes only brought more problems and quality soon began to suffer. The situation continued to decline as the United States entered a recession in the mid-seventies and AMF leadership—increasingly dependent on Harley-Davidson sales to support other lagging businesses—rushed bikes out the door.

Harley-Davidson leadership felt increasingly alienated from the decision makers at AMF, who had little personal investment in the motorcycle business. "The message [from AMF] was 'Get the revenue, we need to maximize sales,'" remembered John Davidson, who served as president of Harley-Davidson from 1973 to 1978 and then chairman of the board through 1981. "That led to pressure to just get bikes out the door. We were actually shipping vehicles out of York with parts missing and asking our dealers to complete the motorcycles. In my judgment, the dealers, God bless 'em, were the key to keeping this whole thing together in that difficult time."

Inevitably, the relationship between AMF and Harley-Davidson began to sour. AMF had expected Harley-Davidson to be a cash cow, delivering a reliable revenue stream and requiring minimal investment, but that just wasn't the case. The firm had underestimated the complexity of the motorcycle industry, and it was spending cubic dollars on new product development in addition to operating and maintenance costs. In 1980, with costs rising and Harley-Davidson's market share falling, AMF decided to put its motorcycle business up for sale.

What happened next was something quite remarkable. On June 16, 1981, thirteen Harley-Davidson executives—including Willie G. Davidson—pooled their resources and bought the company back, returning the brand to enthusiast hands. This was an incredibly risky move: the national economy was in recession, motorcycle sales were plunging, and the new owners were heavily leveraged to secure the total purchase price of $81.5 million.

But at the time, an employee buyback was seen as the only way to save the company. "If we hadn't gone ahead with the purchase of the company, we would have sealed its doom," said Vaughn Beals,

then CEO of the newly reformed Harley-Davidson. "AMF had lost the will to fight for Harley-Davidson's share of the market. It's a heavy responsibility: we make our own decisions now, and if we're wrong, the company could go down the drain."

The new owners set straight to work reviving the company, reenergizing employees, and restoring the faith of its loyal customers. Step one was symbolic: a commemorative "buyback ride" from York to Milwaukee, led by the thirteen executives, who were joined by dealers and press. Step two was ritualistic: the issuing of a detailed memo describing exactly how the AMF logo should be excised from all the tank badges of all new bikes in production. Step three was practical: a comprehensive overhaul of the entire business to implement the latest manufacturing and management techniques to improve quality and further reduce costs.

Employees, dealers, and suppliers were all called upon to assist in the recovery effort, but the biggest changes occurred at the manufacturing level. Harley-Davidson carefully studied the methods of its very successful Japanese competitors and quickly adapted their best techniques, including "just-in-time" inventory management, employee-led problem solving, and greatly enhanced quality-control measures. It all worked, with productivity rising, costs falling, and quality greatly improving.

By 1984, the Motor Company seemed to be on a roll, but the recovery almost flat-lined in 1985. The US economy was in its worst recession in decades, and the motorcycle market was devastated. Not even a tariff imposed on Japanese imports was enough to stave off the almost-daily threat of bankruptcy that loomed over the deep-in-debt company. The situation got critical in late 1985, when the bank that had financed the bulk

of the Motor Company's debt threatened to call the note and begin liquidating company assets. Amazingly, Harley-Davidson—buoyed by public confidence in the skill and dedication of company employees and boosted by a supportive US government—was able to fend off bankruptcy at the last moment and receive a new lease on life in the form of another public stock offering in June of 1986.

"Only in America can a company go from the threat of bankruptcy in December of 1985, to a public company on July 7th of 1986," said Rich Teerlink, then Harley-Davidson CFO. "We went public to get away from the banks. I'd rather deal with a public shareholder than a lender."

Harley-Davidson announced that initial public offering with a full-page ad in *The New York Times*; a second offering on July 1, 1987, in conjunction with the company's listing on the New York Stock Exchange, was even more successful, raising an additional $18 million. The New York Stock Exchange listing was the first signal that

the company's turnaround was complete. The second signal was a visit to the York manufacturing plant on May 6, 1987, by US President Ronald Reagan, who congratulated employees and executives on the company's historic turnaround.

"When it comes to motorcycles, this is the home of the all-American A-team," Reagan remarked. "Of course, that's not what a lot of people were saying about you just a few years ago. Some people said you couldn't make the grade. They said you couldn't keep up with foreign competition. They said Harley-Davidson was running out of gas and sputtering to a stop." Of course, "they" were dead wrong.

Against all odds, the new owners saved Harley-Davidson from suffering the same fate as every other US motorcycle manufacturer in history. Not only that, they built Harley-Davidson into one of the most successful, profitable, and fast-growing corporations in the United States over the past three decades. And it all began with this humble felt-tip pen.

35

HARLEY OWNERS GROUP

The group of thirteen executives who liberated Harley-Davidson from AMF ownership in 1981 had more than enough challenges just trying to improve the manufacturing processes, quality control, and labor issues that had all degraded during twelve years of outside ownership. But there was one thing that was even more important than product—and that was people. Perhaps the greatest challenge the Motor Company's new owners faced during this period was restoring the faith of Harley-Davidson's customers, many of who felt bitter and even betrayed after more than a decade of neglect.

It was toward that end that the Harley Owners Group—colloquially known by the abbreviation HOG—was formed in January of 1983, with the express purpose of strengthening the Motor Company's connection to its customers and building a culture that celebrates the singular sense of camaraderie that comes with Harley-Davidson ownership. "To Ride and Have Fun" is the official HOG motto, and though the group has since expanded far beyond its original mission to now include everything from charity outreach (often in conjunction with the Muscular Dystrophy Association) to a massive merchandise line, that fundamental ethos of two-wheeled fun remains at its core.

The items featured here are the molds used to cast the original Harley Owners Group membership pins. Collecting pins, of course, is a huge part of HOG culture. Many members ride thousands of miles each year just to visit "pin stops" at major motorcycle events, where they receive a special commemorative pin celebrating the occasion. HOG has produced hundreds—if not thousands—of commemorative pins over the past three-plus decades, collecting as many as possible is a priority for many HOG members.

The Harley Owners Group launched in 1983 with just five chapters. Memberships were included with the purchase of all new models, and by the end of that first year, more than thirty thousand people had signed up. Dealer-sponsored local chapters formed by 1985, and today, chapters around the world boast a family of over one million members—making the Harley Owners Group the largest factory-sponsored riding club in the world.

36

THE FIRST SOFTAIL

It's such a signature styling element, the clean, unadorned, rigid rear triangle that defines the back half of almost every early Harley-Davidson from the JD to the iconic EL to the very first FL. Even after the 1958 Duo Glide rendered rigid rear triangles obsolete on production bikes, the "hardtail" remained the frame of choice in the custom motorcycle world. Bike builders couldn't get enough of the simple style and the tough-as-nails street cred that riding a rigid motorcycle conferred.

Bill Davis, an avid biker and mechanical engineer from St. Louis, Missouri, was one of those guys. He loved the rigid chopper look, but he also liked to take long trips and he couldn't handle the harsh ride. So, like any mechanically minded tinkerer, Davis started to experiment on his own 1972 Super Glide—the bike shown here—eventually fabricating a custom swingarm that looked exactly like a rigid rear triangle in profile, but concealed a pair of shock absorbers hidden beneath the rider's seat. The result was a bike that looked to all the world like a vintage hardtail but offered 3 inches of spine-saving rear wheel travel.

Davis proceeded to ride this prototype everywhere, and everywhere he went, people fell in love with it. He considered starting his own company to manufacture aftermarket frames, but then he had another, better thought—why not see if Harley-Davidson was interested in licensing the design? Davis set up a meeting with Willie G in August of 1976 and showed the famed designer his work. Willie G was impressed—and very interested—but Harley-Davidson's engineering department simply didn't have any available bandwidth at the time, and the conversation stalled.

Davis wasn't one to wait around. He went back to the drawing board and designed a second evolution that relocated the shock absorbers from under the seat to beneath the transmission, which allowed him to lower the seat a few more inches and also use a standard Harley-Davidson horseshoe oil tank for a more traditional look. This new version worked even better, inspiring Davis and two partners to found a company called Road Worx and patent what they dubbed the "Sub Shock" frame.

But before the first Road Worx ad in *Easyriders* magazine even appeared on newsstands, Davis and his partners had a falling out, and the company dissolved. The split was so acrimonious that Davis lost all interest in continuing the frame-building business. The brilliant design was in danger of being lost forever—until one day when Jeff Bleustein, then Harley-Davidson's vice president of engineering, called Davis and worked out a deal that would pay Davis a generous royalty on each bike built. Davis sold his patents, the prototype pictured here, and his tooling to Harley-Davidson in January of 1982. And so, the Harley-Davidson Softail was born.

Harley-Davidson barely altered Davis's basic design—the fundamental engineering was that sound. The new platform debuted in dealerships as the 1984 FXST Softail. Basically a Wide Glide with a different rear end, the first Softail nailed the factory chopper look with widely spaced front forks, skinny 21-inch front wheel, forward controls, and the classic hardtail look, but with none of the punishing ride. The FXST was also one of the very first models to be equipped with the all-new, all-aluminum Evolution V-twin engine, which was a huge improvement over aged, cast-iron Shovelhead.

Everything about the first Softail was good, and it was an instant sales success. Despite its $7,999 price tag—Harley-Davidson's

most expensive non-touring model that year—the Softail outsold every other Big Twin in the lineup, boosting sales by a substantial 31 percent. Building off of this success, Harley-Davidson added more and more Softail variations with each successive year—fat-fendered Heritage Softails, muscular-looking Fat Boys, nostalgic Springer Softails, even more factory choppers like the Night Train and the Deuce—and the Softail platform has remained a strong seller ever since.

The Softail has such strong brand equity, in fact, that when the Motor Company decided to streamline its product lineup and combine Dyna and Softail models into a single family for 2018, that family retained the Softail name. All new 2018 models maintained the signature faux-hardtail frame design too, though interestingly, the latest Softail frame has been redesigned to be lighter and stiffer by virtue of utilizing a single shock mounted underneath the seat—very much like Bill Davis's original, first-generation design. This seems poetic—Davis's original design was inspired by earlier Harley-Davidsons, so it makes sideways sense that Harley-Davidson's latest design would be inspired by Davis's earlier work.

The 2018 SOFTAIL CHASSIS,
FIT WITH THE MILWAUKEE-
EIGHT ENGINE.

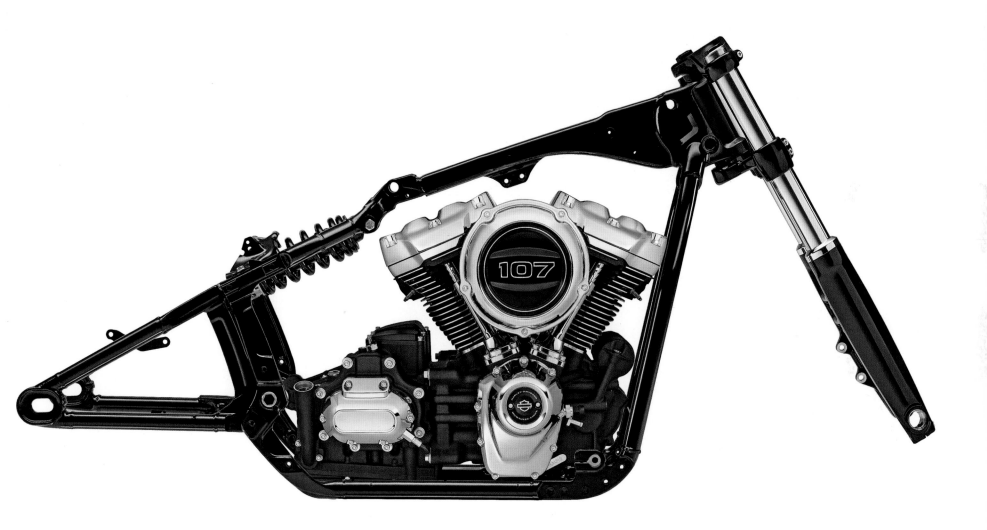

HARLEY-DAVIDSON AND HOLLYWOOD

Read the following in a thick Austrian accent: "I need your clothes, your boots, and your motorcycle."

It's the most memorable scene in *Terminator 2: Judgment Day*. Arnold Schwarzenegger—playing a just-formed android called the Terminator—strides naked into a rowdy biker bar and, after a brutal brawl, takes possession of one thug's leather motorcycle outfit. Then, walking through the parking lot outside, he uses his augmented-reality visual scanning abilities to quickly assess the assembled vehicles and choose his perfect getaway. After considering and then rejecting a series of possibilities including a Ford Crown Victoria, a Yamaha motorcycle, and a few lesser Harley-Davidsons, he makes his choice—a 1990 Harley-Davidson Fat Boy—and roars off into the darkness to save civilization from imminent nuclear annihilation.

Terminator 2 was the highest-grossing film of 1991; in fact, it was the highest-grossing film of Schwarzenegger's legendary acting career. It was the film that catapulted him from star to superstar status, and the film had the same effect on Harley-Davidson's Fat Boy model. And make no mistake—the Fat Boy was very much a star of this movie. Unlike today, when most motorcycles you see in movies are the result of paid product placements, *Terminator 2* director James Cameron specifically cast the Fat Boy for this role. Cameron was undoubtedly drawn to the Fat Boy's muscular good looks—which complemented Schwarzenegger's own broad shoulders—and its

futuristic spun-steel disc wheels. The thunderous roar of the powerful Evolution V-twin engine probably helped too.

Cameron's selection says a lot about the cultural significance of Harley-Davidson during the early 1990s—the beginning of an incredible run of boom years—and the major cultural currency that the Harley-Davidson brand conveyed at that time. There was simply no other vehicle that telegraphed "badass superhero" better than the all-American Fat Boy. And such prominent billing beside the world's greatest action hero paid off greatly for the brand too, making Harley-Davidson impossibly cool and acting as a huge driver of Fat Boy sales. Not every man could have the Terminator's bulging biceps, or his uncanny ability to avoid death. But anyone could stroll down to the nearest Harley-Davidson dealership and purchase the Terminator's motorcycle. His jacket and boots too.

The Harley-Davidson/Hollywood connection goes back much further

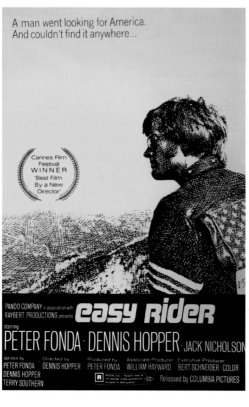

than the 1990s, of course, and the expertly curated "movies and music" gallery inside the museum captures this long and mutually beneficial relationship in great detail beginning with *The Wild One*, released in 1953. Though Marlon Brando's main protagonist Johnny Strabler rides a Triumph Thunderbird, the vast majority of his Black Rebels Motorcycle Club cohorts ride Harley-Davidsons, and their appearance cast the mold for the outlaw biker image that has dominated American motorcycle culture ever since.

This iconic depiction continued to expand throughout the 1960s, thanks to an almost endless series of low-budget "B-movies" that equally celebrated and vilified biker culture—flicks such as *Wild Angels*, *She-Devils on Wheels*, *The Glory Stompers*, and basically the entire

Roger Corman filmography—before the next seismic cultural shift in 1969, with the appearance of the film *Easy Rider*. This cult classic film, starring Peter Fonda and Dennis Hopper and their custom Harley-Davidson choppers nicknamed *Captain America* and the *Billy Bike*, followed two hippie-era dropouts on a meandering road trip searching for an idyllic America that no longer existed. Considered a landmark film and a touchstone for a generation, *Easy Rider* launched the "New Hollywood" era of filmmaking and made those two choppers pop-culture icons and emblems of the rebellious 1960s.

The enduring popularity of Harley-Davidson motorcycles in Hollywood blockbusters—most recently, in the series of movies inspired by Marvel Comics, including the *Captain America* franchise—is just more proof of Harley-Davidson's incredible reversal of fortunes following the company's near-death experience in the early 1980s. It's also proof that the company sells more than just motorcycles—Harley-Davidson is in the business of selling dreams, just like the movies its motorcycles appear in.

38

DESIGN LAB

How is a new Harley-Davidson motorcycle created? That's the subject of the museum's Design Lab exhibit, and as such, it represents a fascinating glimpse behind the curtain at a portion of the Motor Company that is usually strictly off-limits to the general public. Knock on the front door at Harley-Davidson's Product Development Center and, unless you're a member of the engineering or design staff, the front door is as far as you'll get. But the Design Lab is the next best thing, giving a thorough look at the design process from start to finish, beginning with CAD drawings and continuing through physical models and rapid-prototype designs.

This 1:1 scale, hand-sculpted clay model of the original Harley-Davidson V-Rod is typical of the type of artifact you might find in the always-changing Design Lab. Even though computer-aided programs have revolutionized vehicle design, there's still no replacement for a full-size, hands-on model like this V-Rod. Digital drawings, no matter how detailed, just don't give the sense of scale and proportion that a designer needs. Designers need something they can stand back and look at, walk around, and touch. And clay remains the preferred modeling medium—it's easy to work with, easy to change, and able to be reworked repeatedly.

This clay model of the V-Rod was first created in 1996, and subsequently modified numerous times before the bike was finally revealed to the public in 2001. And clay is not a completely retrograde medium either: clay models can now be scanned, converting the hand-shaped form into a digital file that can be manipulated by computer for further development.

The museum collection also includes a full-scale model of the V-Rod's Revolution engine that was made using a laminated object manufacturing (LOM) process where a laser cuts parts from sheets of built-up paper. Modeling technology has changed radically over the years. Previously, if stylists wanted to experiment with a form or modify an existing part, they would engage a model maker who would fabricate a shape by hand from wood or metal or fiberglass. Now they use rapid prototyping machines that can produce a model sometimes in just a few hours, using techniques like stereolithography (SLA), where a laser hardens a photo-sensitive resin, and selective laser sintering (SLS), where a laser fuses thin layers of powdered nylon to produce parts. Both processes are widely used by Harley-Davidson engineers.

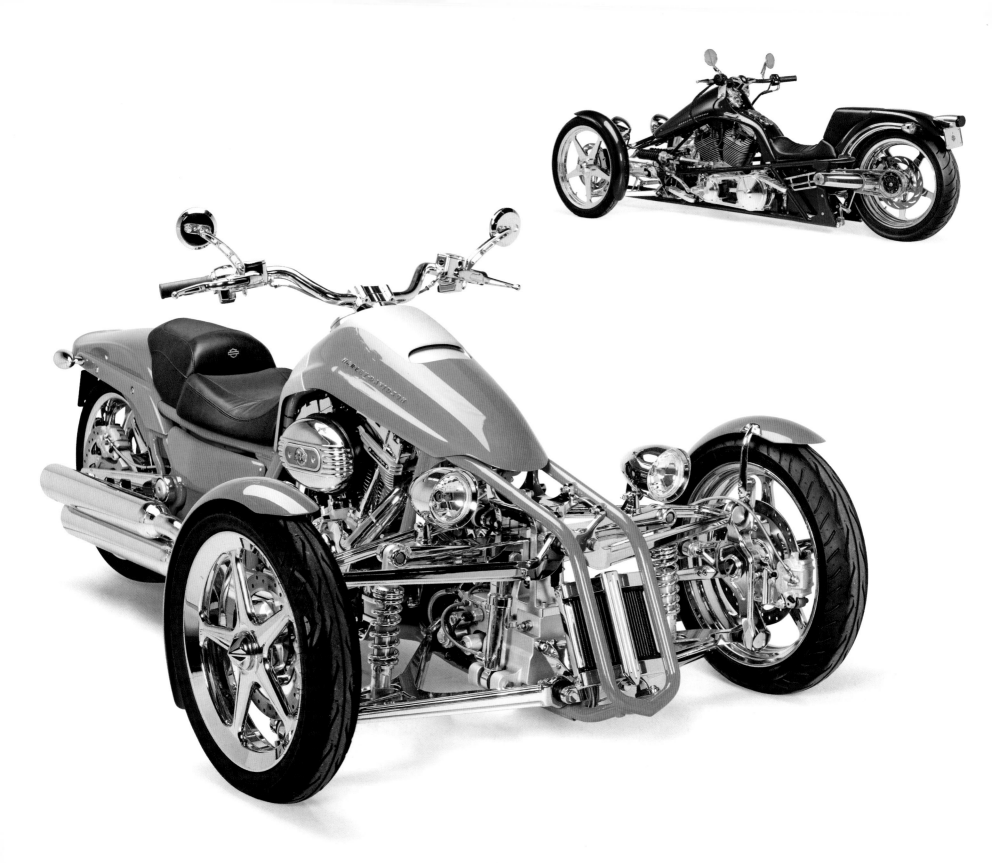

39

PENSTER REVERSE TRIKE

Harley-Davidson is no stranger to three-wheeled vehicles. The Motor Company debuted the Forecar, a reverse trike with dual front wheels and a single rear wheel, way back in 1914. The firm's first conventional trike, the Servi-Car, appeared in 1932.

More than five decades later, in 1985, Harley-Davidson purchased a company called Hawk Vehicles that produced a reverse trike called the Trihawk. Powered by a 1299cc Citroen automobile engine and featuring side-by-side seating and front-wheel drive, the Trihawk was intended as a way for Harley-Davidson diversify its product offerings. But the Trihawk project was stillborn; struggling to rebuild its core motorcycle business at the time, Harley-Davidson simply didn't have the resources to develop the vehicle properly and the Trihawk program was soon cancelled.

The dream of a three-wheeled Harley-Davidson vehicle didn't die with the Trihawk, however. In an attempt to appeal to aging baby boomers who either didn't want to or weren't able to balance a two-wheeled motorcycle, Harley-Davidson developed this unique reverse trike called the Penster, in 1998. Unlike the Trihawk, which was more like a small car than a motorcycle, the Penster is basically a conventional V-twin motorcycle—complete with

handlebar steering—equipped with dual front wheels. The Penster predates the similarly configured Can-Am Spyder by almost a decade, but unlike the single-plane Spyder, the Penster's front wheels actually lean into turns to provide a more dynamic and motorcycle-like riding experience.

The Penster's independent front suspension is very sophisticated, utilizing a computer-controlled, electro-hydraulic assisted steering system to control the leaning front wheels. There are two Pensters in the museum collection: the initial concept from '98, designed and built on contract by legendary hot-rod builder "Lil John" Buttera, and an orange-and-chrome '06 version that is one of four constructed during the Penster's fifth and final development cycle. This highly refined, production-intent three-wheeler shows just how close the Penster came to market, before it was cancelled to make way for the less risky, more conventional Tri Glide trike that was eventually released in 2009.

40

RED MOON LEATHER MOTORCYCLE

Not all of the "motorcycles" in the Harley-Davidson Museum are made of metal. One of the more unique bikes in the collection is made from nearly all leather, though there are steel parts underneath. This 1-scale chopper sculpture was a gift to the museum from the owner and founder of Red Moon, a high-end leather goods manufacturer in Japan.

It took a team of twenty leather artisans almost two years to complete the six-foot-long chopper, and the level of detail is nothing short of remarkable. The Evolution motor is a perfect replica, right down to the exact number of cooling fins. The drive chain is fabricated from individual links and the leather tool pouch mounted to the fork even contains a full set of leather tools. Upon completion in 2001, the Red Moon owner and a few of the workers who contributed to the project flew to Harley-Davidson to personally deliver the sculpture and present it to museum staff.

Creating such a special tribute like Red Moon has done is just one example of the extremely powerful and personal connection so many enthusiasts have with the Harley-Davidson brand. Enthusiasts often want to give something back to Harley-Davidson, and they want to express their passion and contribute to the museum collection in their own unique way. Whether that contribution takes the form of personalized scrapbooks or one-of-a-kind club sweaters or custom bikes like King Kong or even a leather sculpture like the one seen here, the Harley-Davidson Museum features many unique and original artifacts that put that customer passion on full display.

41

TIME TO CELEBRATE

When Harley-Davidson marked its 100th Anniversary in 2003, the company had good reason to celebrate. One hundred years of continuous production was almost fifty years longer than the next longest-lived American motorcycle manufacturer. (Indian's original incorporation lasted fifty-two years, from 1901 to 1953, followed by fifty-eight years of effective dormancy until Polaris acquired the brand in 2011.)

And it certainly wasn't an easy one hundred years, filled with great successes but also tough challenges and even a near-death experience or two. When the century mark rolled around and the Harley-Davidson brand was both stronger and more secure than at any other point in its history, it was time to party.

The invitation was broadcast around the world, and on the last weekend of August in 2003, an estimated 250,000 Harley-Davidson enthusiasts from around the globe arrived in Milwaukee to wish happy birthday to America's favorite motorcycle manufacturer. The homecoming celebration in Milwaukee was the culmination of a year-long Open Road Tour that got revved up with smaller weekend festivals in ten locations around the world, including Sydney, Hamburg, Atlanta, Baltimore, Los Angeles,

Toronto, Dallas, Mexico City, Tokyo, and Barcelona. More than one thousand HOG enthusiasts traveled to Milwaukee from Australia alone, with almost half of them shipping their motorcycles to the northern hemisphere just for the event.

The 100th Anniversary Ride Home invited Harley-Davidson enthusiasts to join one of four rides—from each of the four corners of the United States—for a massive homecoming road trip that included festivities in twenty-six major American cities along the way. In addition to celebrating their passion for Harley-Davidson motorcycles, Anniversary Ride Home participants also raised over $5 million for the Motor Company's charity of choice, the Muscular Dystrophy Association.

Entertainment in Milwaukee included demo rides on the full line of one hundredth anniversary edition motorcycles, all finished with special paint schemes and commemorative badging, as well as stunt shows, plant tours, and live entertainment on ten stages—though the headlining performance by soft-rocker Elton John was a bust, given such a hard-rocking crowd. Much more successful was the formal parade, which included more than ten thousand bikes roaring through downtown Milwaukee in perhaps the longest line of horsepower and chrome-plated hardware that the world has ever seen.

Though the one hundredth anniversary was by far the biggest, it wasn't the first historical occasion observed by Harley-Davidson. That would be the fiftieth anniversary, celebrated with special paint schemes and a commemorative badge on the front fender of all 1954 models—curious, since the first Harley-Davidson was built in 1903. The anniversary editions were revived by AMF in 1978, to celebrate the seventy-fifth anniversary (note the math had been corrected), but it wasn't until the eighty-fifth anniversary in 1988 that the celebrating got serious.

The company had narrowly avoided bankruptcy just three years earlier, but by 1988, it was enjoying a remarkable recovery and company officials wanted to thank the loyal customers who had seen them through hard times. This was the first of the now-traditional "homecoming" events in Milwaukee, and it attracted tens of thousands of enthusiasts. These "five-year" celebrations continued to build in popularity, with the ninety-fifth anniversary homecoming in 1998 drawing nearly one hundred thousand fans of the brand.

The Harley-Davidson Motor Company continues to celebrate its rich and storied history—and the human connection that history creates—with an every-five-year homecoming event in Milwaukee. The anniversary parties reinforce the unifying power of Harley-Davidson motorcycles to bring people from all walks of life, and from every portion of the globe, together to celebrate a shared passion. Harley-Davidson ownership is a membership card into an instant community of like-minded, freedom-loving individuals. More than stylish new models or innovative technology, that's the driving force behind Harley-Davidson's continued popularity, and the key to its continued viability into the next one hundred years.

42

ICONIC PARTNERSHIPS

The Fender Stratocaster guitar is basically the instrumental equivalent of the 1948 Harley-Davidson Hydra-Glide—it's the guitar that shaped the face of early rock-and-roll and the one that still profoundly influences sound and style today, more than six decades later.

Designed in 1954 by Leo Fender, the Stratocaster has been manufactured continuously since its introduction. Its distinctive, double-cutaway shape and its peerless sound quality have made it one of the best-selling and most-copied guitar shapes ever made. The list of Stratocaster players is like a who's who of rock-and-roll: Buddy Holly, Jimi Hendrix, Bob Dylan, Eric Clapton, Dick Dale, George Harrison and John Lennon, Stevie Ray Vaughan, even Eddie Van Halen. If there is one essential, elemental guitar shape in the world, it's the Fender Stratocaster.

So, it's not coincidental that when Harley-Davidson sought other iconic American brands to partner with to draw additional attention to its 105th anniversary in 2008, Fender was at the top of this list. To help celebrate, the Fender Custom Shop was commissioned to create a special-edition Harley-Davidson 105th Anniversary Stratocaster guitar. Fender Custom Shop Craftsmen meticulously handcrafted three identical Stratocaster guitars, each incorporating numerous features that reflect the classic Harley-Davidson design aesthetic. Designed and built by

Custom Shop veteran Scott Buehl, these jet-black guitars were detailed with black-cherry pinstriping, black-chrome and black-nickel hardware, a black polycarbonate Harley-Davidson neck inlay, a jack plate engraved with the Harley-Davidson bar-and-shield logo, a serialized neck plate, perforated alloy pick guards, and more.

The first 105th anniversary commemorative Stratocaster guitar was auctioned online to benefit the Muscular Dystrophy Association, where it sold for $35,088. The second was donated to the then-new Harley-Davidson Museum, to celebrate its grand opening. The third guitar was sent directly to the Fender Museum in Corona, California, where it likewise remains on display today. The creation of these very special guitars exemplifies the increasing importance of the Motor Company's five-year anniversaries and the growing power of the Harley-Davidson brand to support and even lift other iconic American brands.

43

TSUNAMI SURVIVOR

Harley-Davidson motorcycles have been ridden to every corner of the earth, but none has ever made a journey quite as remarkable as this 2004 Night Train once owned by Ikuo Yokoyama, from Miyagi Prefecture, Japan. Yokoyama had his beloved Harley-Davidson Softail parked in a storage container outside his home near the city of Sendai when the devastating, 8.9-magnitude Tohoku earthquake struck on March 11, 2011. The resulting 25-foot tsunami destroyed the twenty-nine-year-old's home and ultimately swept the storage container out to sea.

Remarkably, the insulated—and therefore buoyant—container remained sealed and afloat, drifting slowly across the Pacific Ocean for more than a year. It eventually washed up and then broke apart on a remote beach on British Columbia's Haida Gwaii Island chain, more than 4,000 miles from Yokoyama's home.

A wandering beachcomber named Peter Mark discovered the bike, and it remained partially buried on the beach for over a month before it could be properly recovered. Harley-Davidson HQ heard about the story from staff at Steve Drane Harley-Davidson in Victoria, British Columbia, who assisted in recovering the bike.

The Motor Company originally offered to repair and return the Softail to Yokoyama, but after assessing the full extent of the damage, it offered a replacement bike instead. Yokoyama declined, and instead asked for the bike to be displayed at the Harley-Davidson Museum in Milwaukee as a tribute to the more than fifteen thousand lives lost in the disaster—including three

members of Yokoyama's family. Harley-Davidson obliged, and the bike is on display at the museum now.

Yokoyama's Night Train is displayed in exactly the condition in which it was recovered, badly rust-ravaged after spending so many weeks marinating in seawater and sand. Interestingly, the condition of the bike is constantly changing, as the natural corrosion process continues daily to decay the metal components. The salt crust that formed on the fuel tank and other major components continues to blossom and create new formations, a process that is being tracked and monitored by museum staff with monthly photo documentation.

The display of the Yokoyama's once-prized motorcycle is an incredibly poignant reminder of the power of nature and the terrible human tragedy that happened on the northern coast of Japan on that fateful day.

44

LIVEWIRE ELECTRIC MOTORCYCLE

Who would have ever guessed that good, old Harley-Davidson—not Honda, not Yamaha, not even BMW—would be the first established motorcycle manufacturer to announce that it was building an all-electric motorcycle? Called Project LiveWire, this sleek, all-electric eBike sent a shockwave through the motorcycle industry when it was revealed in 2014 and served as concrete evidence of just how focused Harley-Davidson was on reinventing itself to remain relevant for the next one hundred years.

"America at its best has always been about reinvention," said Matt Levatich, Harley-Davidson President and COO, upon release of the LiveWire. "Like America, Harley-Davidson has reinvented itself many times in our history, with customers leading us every step of the way. Project LiveWire is another exciting, customer-led moment in our history."

Following fast on the heels of the super-stylish Dark Custom series and the affordable and accessible Street lineup, Project LiveWire was the latest salvo in Harley-Davidson's both-barrels-blazing effort to attract new, young, and different customers to the bar-and-shield brand. Not only was the LiveWire's electric drivetrain cutting edge, the styling was a distinct departure from Harley-Davidson's usual cruiser and touring bikes, with a muscular, athletic style not traditionally associated with the Motor Company.

Such avant-garde styling, of course, was entirely on purpose. The LiveWire was a development prototype designed specifically to gather input about riders' expectations for an electric Harley-Davidson motorcycle. (Did anyone have any expectations for an electric Harley-Davidson?) Building upon what was learned from the Project Rushmore touring bike revision from the year previous—overwhelmingly led by the "voice of the customer"—Harley-Davidson was soliciting an unprecedented amount of consumer input into the development of its first electric motorcycle.

⅓-SCALE CLAY MODEL
DEPICTING ELECTRIC
BIKE CONCEPT

For the entire summer of 2014, consumers across the country were given the opportunity to demo ride the LiveWire at more than thirty Harley-Davidson dealers—or participate in a simulated riding experience—and give feedback that would directly shape the future of Harley-Davidson's eBike development. "Longer-term plans for retail availability of Project LiveWire will be influenced by feedback from riders along the Project LiveWire Experience tour," the company said at the time.

Harley-Davidson released very little technical data about the LiveWire at the time, only promising "tire-shredding acceleration" and a unique "fighter jet" sound unlike any internal combustion motorcycle. The LiveWire rolled on 17-inch wheels fit with disc brakes front and rear, and suspension consisted of a substantial inverted fork and centrally mounted rear monoshock—all current sportbike technology. The performance backed up the styling, impressing journalists with thrilling acceleration that delivered a 0–60 time around four seconds and a top speed of over 100 miles per hour.

Harley-Davidson's risky leap into the electric space was immediately rewarded—the reveal of the LiveWire electric motorcycle prototype was the biggest story ever for the Harley-Davidson Motor Company, capturing more column inches, clicks, and overall impressions than any other story in the company's then-111-year history. But after that original the demo tour in the summer of 2014 was over, the LiveWire disappeared almost as quickly as it appeared. Nothing was said about LiveWire plans for almost four years—until early 2018, when Harley-Davidson announced unexpectedly that its first electric motorcycle would be enter production within eighteen months.

Aimed squarely at young motorcycle enthusiasts who are inspired more by Teslas than Trans Ams, the forthcoming electric Harley-Davidson represents a new era for the venerable Motor Company, and another chance to take the lead and define the next 100-plus years of motorcycle style and technology.

45

SERENGETI PROTOTYPE

There's an acronym for everything in engineering, and in this case the acronym is "RTLC." That stands for "Road to Track to Lab to Computer," and it's a brief description of the process sequence every brand-new Harley-Davidson motorcycle follows from prototype through final production. New-model development typically begins with data collection on the road, followed by extensive on-track testing at Harley-Davidson's private test tracks either at Talladega, Alabama, or the Arizona Proving Ground at Yucca, Arizona. The real-world data gathered on road and track is used to program the testing simulators—the dyno cells and shaker tables—at Harley-Davidson's Product Development Center, which run 24/7 to put the equivalent of many thousands of miles of use on a new part in just a matter of a few days or weeks. The results of this lab testing are what inform the final production files that ultimately guide the manufacturing process.

Though it's far from pretty—covered in sensors, strung with bare wires and hung with multiple black-box data collection devices—this Project Serengeti development prototype, one of the most recent additions to the Museum collection, helps visualize this very important story about how Harley-Davidson motorcycles are made. Project Serengeti is the internal code name for the latest 2018 Softail. Dating from around 2015, this particular Serengeti development bike features an early generation of the monoshock frame and Milwaukee-Eight V-twin engine, disguised beneath familiar, Heritage Classic-style bodywork. Harley-Davidson

uses test mules like this to gather two discrete data sets: thermal conditions and movement patterns. This particular test bike is wired for thermal testing, with individual temperature sensors on nearly every possible surface; other test units are rigged with motion sensors that gather suspension and chassis data.

Computer modeling and finite element analysis are essential when developing a new product, of course, but just like stylists still rely on clay models in addition to computer-aided design to see how a shape actually behaves in natural light (see Chapter 38), production engineers similarly rely on real-world data to simulate and recreate riding conditions that a computer can't reliably predict. The accuracy of this programming is quite remarkable.

Test engineers familiar with the Arizona Proving Grounds, for example, can observe a prototype lashed to a shaker table and narrate the ride with stunning accuracy: "right there, the bike just crossed the train tracks outside the main entrance . . ."

It may seem tedious, this painstaking process of gathering data, programming testing equipment and gathering results, but this is how modern Harley-Davidson motorcycles are perfected and so this is an important story to tell. This Serengeti prototype is something very few people have ever seen—and something few other motorcycle makers are willing to share with the public—making it an excellent and very appropriate addition to the Museum collection.

The 2018 Harley-Davidson Fat Bob features the frame and engine developed on the Serengeti prototype.

INDEX

ACKNOWLEDGEMENTS

The Harley-Davidson Museum would like to thank photographer Jim Moy, who worked tirelessly with Museum staff on photography for this book, as well as Jeff Lendrum and Randy Leffingwell, whose work on previous projects has been utilized here. Harley-Davidson Archives Manager Bill Jackson, Senior Archivist Kimberly Thomas, and Archives Technician Katie Simpson all made critical contributions at different stages of book development. None of this would have been possible but for the dedication of Harley-Davidson's founders and the generations of employees who built this company, and their foresight and perseverance in maintaining the materials that provide the foundation of this book.

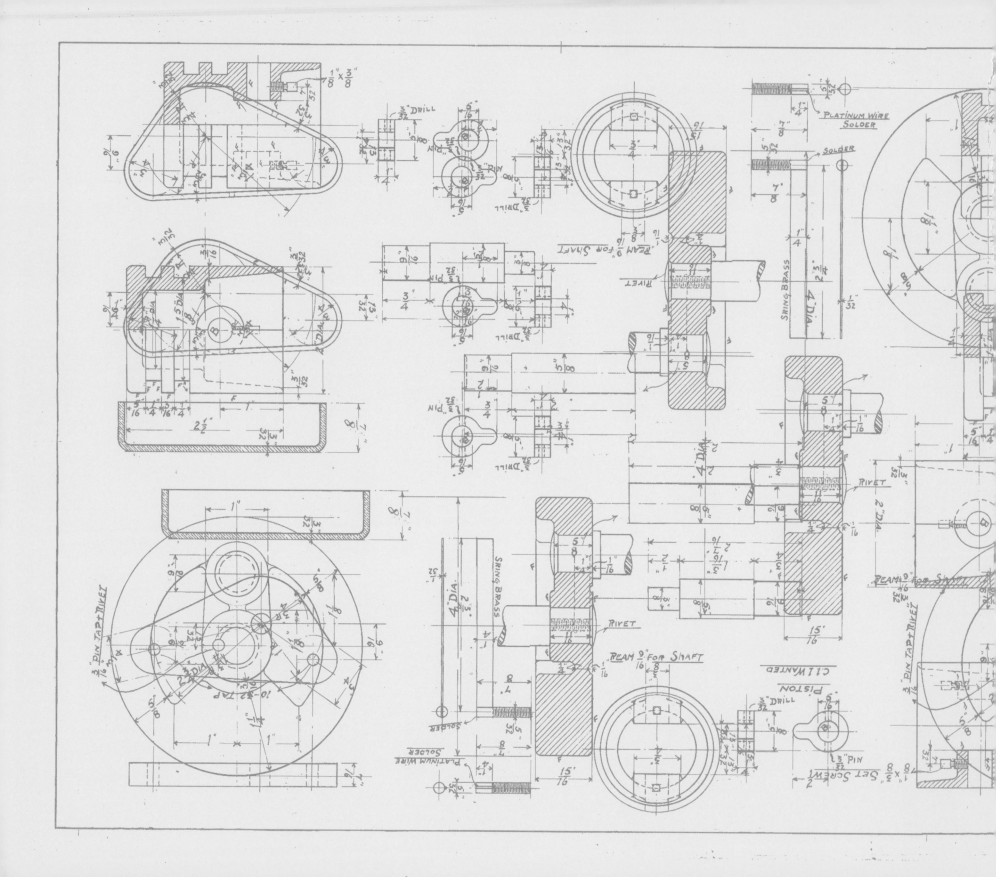